I0148461

Mattie M Jones

The Hygienic Cook-Book; containing recipes for making bread, pies, puddings, mushes, and soups, with directions for cooking vegetables, canning fruit, etc

To which is added an appendix, containing valuable suggestions in regard to washing, bleaching

Mattie M Jones

The Hygienic Cook-Book; containing recipes for making bread, pies, puddings, mushes, and soups, with directions for cooking vegetables, canning fruit, etc
To which is added an appendix, containing valuable suggestions in regard to washing, bleaching

ISBN/EAN: 9783744789233

Printed in Europe, USA, Canada, Australia, Japan

Cover: Foto ©Lupo / pixelio.de

More available books at **www.hansebooks.com**

THE

HYGIENIC COOK-BOOK;

CONTAINING

RECIPES FOR MAKING BREAD, PIES, PUDDINGS, MUSHES,
AND SOUPS, WITH DIRECTIONS FOR COOKING
VEGETABLES, CANNING FRUIT, ETC.

TO WHICH IS ADDED

AN APPENDIX,

CONTAINING VALUABLE SUGGESTIONS IN REGARD TO WASHING,
BLEACHING, REMOVING INK, FRUIT, AND OTHER STAINS
FROM GARMENTS, ETC.

BY MRS. MATTIE M. JONES.

NEW-YORK:
MILLER & BROWNING, PUBLISHERS,
NO. 15 LAIGHT STREET.
1864.

Entered according to act of Congress, in the year 1864, by

MILLER & BROWNING,

In the Clerk's Office of the District Court of the United States for the Southern
District of New York.

L. H. BIGAREL, PRINTER, HYGIENIC INSTITUTE, NEW YORK.

PREFACE.

THE table! how vast an influence it exerts on human life and character; how much of the weal or woe of humanity clusters around it! In determining our physical, mental, and moral conditions, no other one thing in all the material universe has so vast a power as that which we take daily in the shape of food and drink.

Much, very much, of the sickness, suffering, and premature death in the world; much of its vice, immorality, and crime, can, if traced to its starting-point, be found to originate here. Anxious days and sleepless nights are spent by parents, in their earnest endeavors to ·devise some means to subdue the peevishness, the fretfulness, the obstinacy or the immorality of their children, only to find alas! their admonitions unheeded, their exhortations thrown to the winds, their agonizing prayers of no avail; they little dreaming that the causes of this perverseness lie, in a great measure, within their own control; that these unhappy mental and moral manifestations are caused by a disordered condition of the bodily functions, produced by the improper kinds and quantities of food which they have allowed them to eat.

That abnormal conditions of the body never exist without more or less influencing the mind, no arguments are needed to prove. Take for instance the drunkard while under the dominion of alcohol. Of what avail are his own resolutions, or the prayers, the tears, the earnest entreaties of friends, to stay the fierce, ungovernable passions which rage within him, or to rouse him from the dull, leaden stupor into which the demon of drink often plunges its victims? What are moral influences then? So many "wisps of straw" to bind the Samson of evil. But, *remove the cause*, then your appeals to his better nature *may* be of some avail; while it remains, never.

It is but speaking the simple truth to say that fully one half the evil and misery which exists in the world, has its origin in improper dietetic habits. The starting-point of intemperance, in ninety-nine cases out of a hundred, is in the stimulating or gross food and drink received at a fond mother's table in infancy and boyhood, producing in time a craving for stronger stimulus, found at last in the intoxicating cup.

And to that table, too, may be traced the origin of a majority of the countless diseases which people our cemeteries, and make this bright world of ours really a "vale of tears."

All over the land are scattered, by hundreds and thousands, wretched invalids—poor, miserable dyspeptics, to whom life is a burden, and existence a bane—consumptives, lingering with one foot in the grave, who to-day might have been doing the work of strong and earnest men and women, had they and their parents but realized the truth of this. And to too many of them, years and years, yea, a lifetime of earnest effort in the "better way," are barely sufficient to undo the wrong which need never have existed.

Health Reform does not seek to curtail the gustatory pleasures of the table, but rather to enhance them. No drunkard can enjoy his glass of brandy as the teetotaler does his cup of clear, cold, sparkling water.

So, those who live upon rich and stimulating food are really losers, instead of gainers, in the pleasures of the table. The spices, condiments and seasonings universally employed, so far destroy the natural flavor of food that the taste of persons habitually accustomed to their use, becomes so perverted, that they can no more detect the real delicate flavor of the food itself, than the drunkard can appreciate the excellence of pure water; and their enjoyment is not to be compared in steady lasting endurance to that of those who live upon a truly hygienic diet, as all who have tried it throughly can testify.

A cook-book containing directions for preparing a variety of hygienic dishes, which shall be at the same time practical, concise, and in a form cheap enough to bring it within the means of every family seems a *desideratum* hitherto unattained.

That this little work may supply this want, and prove of practical value to those desirous of learning a more healthful method of living, is the earnest wish of

THE AUTHOR.

THE HYGIENIC COOK-BOOK.

BREAD AND BREAD-MAKING.

As by common consent Bread is the "Staff of Life," the question naturally arises, "what are the best methods of making it?" The common white flour fermented bread, which is so universally used, is very far from being the best as an article of diet. The use of fine or bolted flour, has opened upon community a perfect "Pandora's Box" of evils in the shape of Constipation and the ten thousand ailments to which it gives rise. By the separation of the bran from the flour, not only a portion of the grain necessary to the proper distension of the stomach and bowels is removed, but it has been repeatedly proved by chemical analysis that the bran is as rich, or richer, in nutritious substances than the flour.

These are not merely the "notions" of "hair-brained," "bran-bread," "crazy fanatics!" but FACTS which commend themselves to the common sense of all who will investigate, which have been proved by the experience of thousands, and which have been demonstrated by the highest scientific authorities, a few of which we qnote :

DR. JOHNSON, M.A., F.R.S., F.G.S., &c., in his "Chemistry of Common Life," says : "The bran or husk of wheat, which is separated from the fine flour in the mill, and is often condemned to humbler uses, is somewhat more nutritious than either the grain as a whole, or the whiter part of the flour. The nutritive quality of any variety of grain depends very much upon the proportion of gluten it contains ; and the proportions of this in the whole grain, the bran and the fine flour respectively, of the same sample of wheat, are very nearly as follows—whole grain, 12 pr. ct. : whole bran, (outer and inner skins), 18 pr. ct. ; fine flour, 10 pr. ct.

If the grain, as a whole, contain more than twelve per cent. of gluten, the bran and the flour will also contain more than is above represented, and in a like proportion. The whole meal obtained by simply grinding the grain is equally nutritious with the grain itself By sifting out the bran, we render the meal less nutritious, weight for weight; and when we consider that the bran is rarely less, and is sometimes considerably more than one-fourth of the whole weight of the grain, we must see that the total separation of the covering of the grain causes much waste of wholesome human food. Bread made from the whole meal is, therefore, more nutritious ; and as many persons find it a more salutary food than white bread, it ought to be more generally preferred and used."

Prof. Youmans, author of the standard works on "Chemistry," " Household Science, "Chemical Chart," etc., says :

"The grain of which bread is made consists mostly of starch, gluten, and sugar. The ligneous husk of grain produces the bran, while the flour is formed by the interior white portions. The gluten is tougher and more difficult to grind than the starch, hence the finest and whitest flour, obtained by repeated siftings, contains a larger proportion of starch, the darker colored flour being richer in gluten ; and as the nutritive properties of flour are in proportion to the nitrogenized element (gluten), the latter will make the most nutritious bread."

The "Eclectic Review," in an article entitled "Frauds in Foods," says :

" Many of the most important elements of our blood, brain and bone are found in the greatest abundance in the colored, outer part of the wheat, which we deem fittest for pigs ; so we fatten them and suffer ourselves. The difference in nourishing properties between whole meal and flour and very finely dressed flour amounts, in many cases, to fully one-third."

Dr. Bennett says :

" Now, if there is a well established fact emanating from chemical analysis, it is this: That superfine or very finely bolted wheat flour will not alone sustain animal life. This fact has been repeatedly demonstrated by Magendi, the greatest physiologist that ever lived. Having ascertained that the muscular and nervous tissues, including the whole brain or cerebral mass, was composed of nitrogenous matter, he readily concluded that starch, or the fecula of wheat, would not alone sustain animal life, for the reason that it contains not a particle of nitrogenous matter. Consequently, he found by experiment, that animals fed exclusively on very finely dressed flour, died in a few weeks, whereas those fed on the unbolted thrived."

Dr. John Ellis, Professor of the Principles and Practice of Medicine, says :

"The worst case of scurvy I ever had to treat, occurred in a little girl five or six years old, who had lived entirely upon toast made of superfine flour."

We might quote many more, but these must suffice.

The second objection to the common method of bread-making is the fermenting process to which it is subjected. Fermentation, as all persons at all conversant with chemistry know, is, as described by Professor Johnson,

"The consequence of a peculiar action which yeast exercises upon moist flour. It first changes a portion of the starch of the flour into sugar, and then converts this sugar into alcohol and carbonic acid, in the same way as it does when it is added to the worts of the brewer or the distiller. As the gas cannot escape from the glutinous dough, it collects within in large bubbles, and makes it swell, till the heat of the oven kills the yeast plant, and causes the fermentation to cease."

Prof. Youmans says:

"If the fermentation proceeds too far, the dough becomes sour; that is, the vinous passes into the acetous fermentation, the alcohol changes to vinegar."

Who would think of taking a half-decayed apple or potato, and subjecting it to the action of heat to stay the process of putrefaction, and then placing it before human beings as food ? And yet this is precisely what is done by fermentation. Take a common bread "sponge," as it is called. Let it remain thirty-six hours longer than usual, and what is the result ? — a sour, almost putrid mass. This process of putrefaction commences the moment the yeast is added to moist flour, and is only checked by the action of heat.

Baker's bread is often still more objectionable, from the fact that an inferior article of flour is used which is disguised by the introduction of alum and other chemicals.

Soda and saleratus, in all their forms, are decidedly injurious, and when introduced into bread, biscuit, and other articles of food, are a prolific source of disease.

Having demonstrated the effects of bad material and management of it, we will consider what are the best materials and the best methods of preparing and cooking them.

Bread, to be the most wholesome and palatable, should contain but two ingredients—unbolted flour from the best quality of wheat or other grain, and pure water. The following, so far as we know, are the preferable methods of making it, arranged in the order of their respective merits :

UNLEAVENED BREAD.

No. 1.—GEMS.—Into cold water stir Graham flour sufficient to make a batter a trifle thicker than that used for ordinary griddle cakes. Bake in a HOT oven in small tin patty-pans two inches square, and three fourths of an inch deep.

NOTE.—This makes delicious bread. No definite rule as to the proportions of flour and water can be given, owing to the difference in the absorbing properties of various brands of flour. Of some kinds, the batter will require to be made considerably stiffer than the consistency above mentioned. A little experience will enable any person to approximate the right proportions with sufficient exactness. The flour should be stirred into the water very slowly in the same manner as in making mush. No more stirring is necessary after the flour is all added. If hard water is used in making them, they are apt to be slightly tough. A small quantity of milk will remedy this defect.

Many persons have failed of sucess in making this bread from neglecting one very essential requisite—the size of the pans in which it is baked. If they are larger than the dimensions given, the bread will be heavy; if smaller it will be dry and hard. But made this size, and filled full, if the flour is properly ground, the batter the right consistency, and the oven hot, (a hot oven being absolutely indispensable to success,) it will rise one half, and be almost as light and porous as sponge cake.

NOTE.—We used separate pans for some time, but found them quite inconvenient. We have them now formed and wired together as represented in the above cut, and find them a very great improvement.

Any tinman can make them, or with less trouble and no more expense, they may be procured of MILLER & BROWNING, No. 15 Laight St., N. Y., who to supply the continued demand for them, have had heavy iron moulds cast to form them, and can supply them at the rate of $1.25 per square of a dozen tins.

No. 2.—DIAMONDS.—Pour boiling water on Graham flour—stirring rapidly till all the flour is wet. Too much stirring makes it tough. It should be about as thick as can be stirred easily with a strong iron spoon. Place the dough with plenty of flour upon the moulding board, and knead it for two or three minutes. Roll out one half an inch thick, and cut in small cakes or rolls. If a large quantity is required, roll about three-fourths of an inch thick, and cut with a knife in diamond shape. Bake in a very hot oven forty-five minutes.

NOTE.— The names by which these two kinds of bread are known in our Institution are merely arbitrary. Years ago the guests of the house christened No. 2 "diamonds," from their shape. No. 1 being of quite recent introduction, and, as many think, much superior, some facetious patient, on their first appearance, suggested "gems" as an appropriate name, and, accordingly, "gems" went the round of the tables till the soubriquet became firmly attached to them.

No. 3.—GRAHAM BISCUIT.—Make Graham mush as for table. When cool, mix with it Graham flour sufficient to roll well. Knead for a few minutes, roll three-fourths of an inch thick, cut with a common biscuit cutter, and bake in a hot oven from thirty to forty-five minutes.

No. 4.—GRAHAM BISCUIT.—(ANOTHER FORM.) Stir into cold water, Graham flour enough for a rather soft dough ; knead it for five or ten minutes, and bake the same as No. 3.

NOTE.—When these have become a little dry or hard, cut in small pieces, cover with cold water, soak till thoroughly soft, when the water should be all absorbed. Strain through a collander, mix Graham flour sufficient to roll, and bake in the same form as at first. This is even superior to the original bread.

No. 5.—WHEAT MEAL CRISPS.—Make a very stiff dough of Graham flour and cold water; knead thoroughly, roll as thin as possible and bake for twenty minutes in a hot oven.

No. 6.—GRAHAM CRACKERS are made by mixing cold water and Graham flour together, and kneading very thoroughly. They can only be well made by the machinery used in cracker bakeries.

RYE AND OAT-MEAL BREAD.

Unbolted rye or oatmeal, prepared after recipe No. 4, makes excellent and wholesome bread for those who like the peculiar flavor of these grains.

CORN CAKE.

Pour 1 quart boiling water on 1 quart corn meal, and stir quickly. Wet the hands and form the dough into small round cakes one-half an inch thick. The addition of a few raspberries, huckleberries, or any subacid fruit, is a decided improvement. Sweet apples, chopped fine, are also excellent.

CORN MEAL GEMS.

Stir slowly into one quart sweet milk, corn meal sufficient to make a very thin batter. Bake in a hot oven in the gem tins.

MUSHES AND PORRIDGES.

Dr. TRALL in his excellent "Hydropathic Cook Book," says:

"For making unleavened bread, mushes, etc., the grain should be carefully cleaned—washed, if necessary—and care should be taken to select that which is full and plump. When ground at an ordinary flouring mill, the stones should be sharp, so as to cut the grain into very fine particles. If ground by dull stones, the bran will be mashed off in flakes or scales. The meal or flour should be fresh ground, and never kept a long time, as it deteriorates surely, though slowly, every day after being ground."

Under the head of Mushes and Porridges, he has given a variety of very excellent recipes. I cannot do better than copy the chapter entire :

"The reader will observe that salt is not mentioned as an ingredient in this book. But as almost all persons are accustomed to the use of this seasoning, I can only say to them, if they cannot bring their appetite at once into subjection to unsalted aliment, they had better use a moderate quantity, and gradually diminish it.

In all the cook books I am acquainted with, salt is put down as a fixture of every dish; and mushes, especially Indian and rice, are usually considered as unendurably flat and insipid, unless abundantly salted. A little experience with unsalted food, and a little self-denial, will, however, enable all persons to relish not only mushes, but all other farinaceous preparations, with no other seasonings than sugar or milk."

"CRACKED WHEAT MUSH.—As the grits swell very much in boiling, they should be stirred gradually in boiling water until a thin mush is formed. The boiling should then be continued very moderately for one or two hours.

If the grits are ground very coarse, they will require boiling five or six hours. A large coffee mill will serve the purpose very well of grinding for a family.

An ordinary iron pot will answer to boil the grits in, if they are constantly stirred, or if the vessel stand on legs, so that the blaze of the fire is not in immediate contact with it. The double boiler, however (found at most hardware stores,) is the most convenient to prevent burning or scorching. It is a tin or iron vessel surrounded by hot water, and contained within another vessel which comes in contact with the fire.

(10)

HOMINY.—This is generally, in this market, prepared from the Southern or white corn, which is cut into coarser or finer particles of nearly uniform size. It is cooked like the wheaten grits, and usually requires to be boiled one hour and a half. The fine-grained hominy can be well cooked in half an hour, by boiling a few minutes and then steaming it, without stirring, over as hot a fire as can be borne without scorching. Two quarts of water are required for one of hominy.

SAMP.—This is merely a very coarse hominy—the grains of corn being cut or broken into very coarse particles. It should be washed several times, and the water poured through a sieve to separate the hulls; and it requires boiling five or six hours.

This is made precisely like the mush of cracked wheat, or wheaten grits. It is particularly adapted to those who have long suffered from habitual constipation. To persons unaccustomed to the grain, the effect on the bowels is decidedly laxative. The meal must be fresh ground, and made of·well-cleaned and plump grain.

INDIAN-MEAL MUSH.—White and yellow corn meal are made into the well-known mush called hasty pudding. Either kind is equally agreeable to most persons. It should be stirred very gradually into boiling water, so as to prevent lumping; it should be cooked from one to two hours.

OATMEAL MUSH.—This, in Scotland, is called "stirabout." It is a favorite with many persons, and makes a pleasant change of dishes. It is cooked precisely like Indian mush.

WHEAT-MEAL MUSH.—This is an excellent article for infants and young children—much better than the farina, which is so extensively employed. It will do for a change in the cases of adults, but is not equal to the coarser preparations of the grain. It is cooked like Indian mush.

FARINA MUSH.—This is too nutrative, or, rather, concentrated, an aliment for an every day dish, but will do occasionally for variety's sake. It is made into mush in the same way as Graham flour or Indian meal.

RICE MUSH.—Put one pint of plump "head rice," previously picked over and washed, into three quarts of boiling water; continue the boiling fifteen or twenty minutes, but avoid stirring it so as to break up or mash the kernels; turn off the water; set it uncovered over a moderate fire, and steam fifteen minutes. Rice is "poor stuff" without salt, say the cooks, and cook-books. If you find it so, reader, try a little syrup or sugar.

RICE AND MILK MUSH.—Boil a pint of clean head rice fifteen or twenty minutes; pour off the water; add a little milk—mixing it gently so as not to break the kernels—and boil a few minutes longer.

CORN STARCH BLANC-MANGE.—Dissolve half a pound of corn starch in a pint of cold milk; then put it into three pints of boiling milk, and boil very moderately five or six minutes.

MOLDED FARINACEA.—Nearly all the boiled farinaceous foods may be molded to please the fancy, in teacups, glasses, or earthen molds. Wheaten grits, rice, farina, corn starch, etc., may be put into the molds, or dishes, previously wet in cold water, as soon as cooked, and when cooled, turn out on china or glass plates. The addition of a little whortleberry, raspberry, blackberry, or strawberry juice, will afford an innocent coloring material for those who have time and inclination to indulge in such amusements.

MILK PORRIDGE.—Place a pint and a half of new milk, and half a pint of water over the fire; when just ready to boil, stir in a table-spoonful of flour, wheat-meal, oatmeal, or corn-meal, previously mixed with a little water; after boiling a minute, pour it on bread cut into small pieces.

WHEAT-MEAL PORRIDGE.—Stir gradually into a quart of boiling water half a pound of wheat-meal, and boil ten or fifteen minutes. It may be flavored with a little milk, molasses, or sugar.

OATMEAL PORRIDGE.—Rub three-quarters of a pound of oatmeal into a little cold water, till the mixture is smooth and even; add it to three pints of boiling water; allow the whole to boil gently about twenty minutes. Serve with milk, syrup, or sugar.

To those who use milk and desire a great variety, we may add that the cracked wheat, rye, oatmeal, farina, and hominy mushes, are by many considered far preferable if made of half milk. The cracked wheat mush is also improved by the addition of a few raisins, cherries, or dates, added at the commencement of the cooking process. A very palatable dish may be made very quickly, by stirring Graham flour into boiling milk, after the manner of hasty pudding, letting it cook for five or ten minutes.

PIES AND PIE CRUSTS.

PIES, as usually made, are among the greatest abominations of modern cookery. The idea of eating a piece of bread an inch in thickness, with from one-quarter to a half or a whole inch of lard or butter would, by every sane person, be considered preposterous. But people use these same proportions of flour and grease in their pastry, thinking it delicious! Consult any of the ordinary cook books, and you will find the recipes for pastry varying from half a pound to a pound of lard or butter to each pound of flour, and white flour at that! Can anything be conceived which is more indigestible?

We give below recipes for making quite a variety of pies, which any cook after a little practice, can succeed in making, provided she has a heart in the work, and desires to see hygienic cooking take the place which it deserves.

POTATO PIE CRUST.—Boil one quart dry, mealy potatoes. The moment they are done mash them, and sift through a collander. Stir thoroughly together one cup Graham flour and one cup white flour, then add the potatoes, rubbing them evenly through the flour in the same manner as the shortening in common pie crust. Have ready one cup corn meal; pour over it one and one-third cups boiling water, stirring it till all the meal is wet, then add it to the potatoes and flour, mixing only till thoroughly incorporated together. No more flour should be added. The moulding board should be well covered with dry flour, however, as it is slightly difficult to roll out. It should be rolled very thin, and baked in a moderate oven.

NOTE.—It is very essential that the above conditions should all be complied with. Bear in mind that the potatoes must be *hot*, and mixed immediately with the flour; the water be poured, while *boiling*, upon the corn meal, and the whole mixed together very quickly and baked immediately. Inattention to any of these requisites will be quite apt to insure a failure.

CREAM PIE CRUST.—Take equal quantities of Graham flour, white flour, and Indian meal; rub evenly together, and wet with very thin sweet cream. It should be rolled thin and baked in an oven as hot as for common pie crust.

NOTE.—This makes excellent pastry if properly baked. Many patients have said to us they did not see how they could ever again relish the pastry in common use (this is so much sweeter and more palatable, to say nothing of its wholesomeness.) It is more generally relished than the potato crust, although not quite so hygienic.

PUMPKIN PIE.—Select a pumpkin which has a deep, rich color, and firm, close texture. Stew and sift in the ordinary manner; add as much boiling milk as will make it about one-third thicker than for common pumpkin pie. Sweeten with equal quantities of sugar and molasses, and bake about one hour in a hot oven.

NOTE.—Those who will try this method will be surprised to find how delicious a pie can be made without eggs, ginger, or spices of any kind. The milk being turned boiling hot upon the pumpkin, causes it to swell in baking, so that it is as light and nice as though eggs had been used.

SQUASH PIE.—This is even superior to pumpkin, as it possesses a richer, sweeter flavor, and is far preferable. It is made in precisely the same manner as pumpkin pie.

SWEET POTATO PIE.—Boil and sift through a collander, nice, ripe, sweet potatoes, add boiling milk, and make the same as pumpkin pie.

SWEET APPLE PIE.—Pare mellow, sweet apples, and grate them upon a grater. A very large grater is necessary for this purpose. Then proceed as for pumpkin pie.

SOUR APPLE PIE.—Take nice, tart apples—spitzenbergs are best, although pippins, greenings, russets, etc., are excellent. Slice them; fill the under crust an inch thick; sprinkle sugar over them; add a spoonful or two of water; cover with a thin crust, and bake three-fourths of an hour in a moderate oven.

PIE-PLANT PIE.—Remove the skin from the stalks; cut them in small pieces; fill the pie dish evenly full; put in plenty of sugar, a teaspoonful of water; dredge a trifle of flour evenly over the top; cover with a thin crust, and bake the same as apple pie.

NOTE.—If the stalks are not very tender, it is better to partially stew before baking.

APPLE AND PIE-PLANT PIE.—Equal quantities of apple and pie plant made in the same manner as all pie plant, make excellent pie.

DRIED WHORTLEBERRY PIE.—To two quarts dried whortleberries add one pint dried plums; look over carefully; add sugar to the taste, and stew as for the table; bake between two crusts about one hour.

DRIED ELDERBERRY PIE—Is made in the same manner, and is nearly as good as the preceding.

GOOSEBERRY PIE.—This is made in precisely the same manner as currant pie; it is very palatable.

CHERRY PIE.—Choose fair, ripe cherries, the large black English being the best for this purpose; wash and look them over carefully; fill the pie plate evenly full; strew sugar over the top; dredge in plenty of flour; cover with a moderately thick upper crust, and bake one hour.

RASPBERRY PIE.—This stands at the head of the list of all berry pies in point of excellence. Take nice ripe berries, either red or black are about equally good; wash and pick them over carefully; place them an inch or more thick on the under crust; strew a small quantity of sugar, and a trifle of flour over them; put on the upper crust, and bake half an hour.

BLACKBERRY PIE.—This is made in the same manner as the preceding. All berries for pies should be ripe or nearly so, and as fresh as possible.

WHORTLEBERRY PIE.—Whortleberries make excellent pies, and are in market usually longer than any of the summer fruits. It is made in the same manner as raspberry pie.

STRAWBERRY PIE.—Is made in the same way also. This fruit is rather acid, and requires considerable sugar to make it pleasant.

CRANBERRY TART.—Wash the berries in a pan of water, rejecting all the bad ones; simmer them till they become soft and burst open; strain through a fine wire seive, removing all the hulls; add sugar to the taste; bake on a thick under crust in a moderate oven.

PEACH PIE.—Select rich, juicy peaches, of a rather small and nearly uniform size. They should be very ripe; wash them thoroughly to remove all the furz; fill the pie dish with them; sprinkle sugar and a little flour over them; add a tablespoonful of water; cover and bake one hour.

NOTE.—If the peaches are not very ripe, it is better to pare, stone, and slice them.

PLUM PIE—Is made in the same manner as the peach pie. It is not as wholesome, as it requires much more sugar to make it at all palatable.

APPLE PUFFS.—Make a crust the same as for cream pie crust, using rather thicker cream, however; roll as thin as possible; cut out in small round cakes with a common biscuit cutter; take one of these, wet it around the edge, and place in the center a teaspoonful of apple sauce. Take another and cut with a small cracker cutter a hole in the center about one inch in diameter; place the ring which is left upon the first one, and pinch the edges tightly together. Bake in a quick oven.

NOTE.—These, if rightly made, are very nice. Any kind of fruit may be used in place of apple sauce, by stewing it, and simmering down till very little juice remains.

CURRANT PIE.—Currants are made into pies by stewing them, and sweetening according to the degree of acidity, and baking between two crusts in the ordinary manner. Or better still, merely fill the pie with them without any previous cooking. Sprinkle sugar over; dredge in a little flour, and bake the same as apple pie.

I have been much more minute in giving these recipes than persons accustomed to cooking would deem at all necessary. I have done so because hundreds of ladies who have no practical knowledge of even the ordinary methods of cookery, are yearly adopting our system, and as they generally find it impossible to obtain help in their own homes who are at all conversant with it, they feel the necessity of learning its details for themselves.

PUDDINGS.

MANY physiologists object, and justly, to the extensive use of puddings as an article of diet. They admit of but very imperfect mastication and insalivation, even in their best forms, and are to be permitted rather than recommended.

However, as people usually demand something as a dessert, occasionally, by way of variety, they are admissible. I give below recipes for the most Hygienic methods of making them. Quite a number of them are copied from Dr. Trall's Hydropathic Cook Book :

RICE PUDDING.—To two-thirds of a cup of rice add half a cup of sugar, half a cup raisins, and two quarts milk. Stir all together and bake very slowly about three hours.

BAKED APPLE PUDDING.—Pare, core, and slice about two quarts nice tart apples. Add to them one teacup full of Indian meal, one cup Graham flour, and stir all together. Pour over them three-fourths of a cup of sugar dissolved in one cup cold water, stirring till all the flour is wet. Strew Indian meal smoothly over the bottom of a deep basin or pan to prevent sticking, and turn the mixture into it, smoothing it evenly over the top. Then spread smoothly over it a batter made by stirring together half a cup cold water, three tablespoonfuls of Indian meal, three ditto of Graham flour, and one tablespoonful sugar. Bake about two hours and a half.

NOTE.—This is to be eaten with sweetened cream or a sauce made by stirring into one quart boiling milk two heaping tablespoonfuls of corn starch, moistened with cold milk, letting it boil for five or ten minutes afterward. Sweeten according to taste.

PLUM PUDDING.—One quart Indian meal, one cup molasses, one cup raisins, one quart boiling water. Stir all together and steam three hours. This is to be eaten with the same kind of sauce as for baked apple pudding.

RUSK PUDDING.—One and one-third cups rusk, half a cup sugar, two cups sweet apples, sliced, two quarts milk. Stir together and bake two hours and a half.

BAKED INDIAN PUDDING.—Two quarts sweet milk, one heaping teacup full of Indian meal, one-third cup molasses, one-third cup sugar. When the milk is boiling hard, dip out one-half of it, and into the remainder stir the meal slowly, taking care that no lumps remain in it. Add the rest of the milk, the sugar and molasses, and bake about two hours, or until it is a bright cherry color. Stir once or twice the first half hour, but not afterward.

This proportion of meal will not hold good in all cases, owing to the difference in the thickening properties of different kinds. Of some it will require one and one-third cups, others one and a half. This can easily be determined by one trial.

SAGO PUDDING.—Two quarts boiling milk, one cup sago, three-fourths cup sugar, two cups sweet apples sliced. Bake one hour and a half.

TAPIOCA PUDDING.—Two quarts milk, one cup tapioca, one cup sugar, two cups sweet apples, sliced. Bake one hour and a half.

SAGO AND APPLE PUDDING.—Take six ounces of sago, previously washed and picked, five large, rich apples, peeled, quartered and cored, and one teacupful of sugar. Pour boiling water on the sago; let it stand till cold; then mix in the apples and sugar, and bake about one hour.

PEARL BARLEY PUDDING.—Pick and wash half a pound of pearl barley; soak it in fresh water over night; pour off the water; add one quart new milk and a teacupful of sugar; and bake one hour in a slow oven.

BARLEY AND APPLE PUDDING.—Pick and wash half a pound of pearl barley; soak it in water twelve hours; then put it into a pan with three pints of water; let it boil ten hours; pour it into a pie dish; put in half a pound of apples, sliced; add two ounces of sugar, and bake one hour in a moderate oven.

BREAD PUDDING.—Pour a quart of boiling milk on as much bread, biscuit or crackers, broken or cut into small pieces, as will absorb it; cover it and let it remain till quite cool; then sweeten and bake an hour and a half.

CRACKED WHEAT PUDDING.—Boil wheaten grits till quite soft; then dilute the mush with milk to the proper consistency. It should be rather thin; sweeten and bake one hour.

HOMINY PUDDING.—Mix cold, boiled hominy with milk till sufficiently diluted; sweeten and bake in a hot oven an hour and a half, or two hours.

HOMINY PUDDING.—(another form.) Into two quarts boiling milk, stir one large cupful of uncooked hominy. Add one half cup sugar, one half cup raisins and bake two hours.

CHRISTMAS PUDDING.—Mix together a pound and a quarter of flour or meal, half a pint of sweet cream, a pound of stoned raisins, four ounces of currants, four ounces of potatoes, mashed, five ounces of brown sugar, and a gill of milk. When thoroughly worked together add eight large spoonfuls of clean snow; diffuse it through the mass as quickly as possible; tie the pudding tightly in a bag previously wet in cold water, and boil four hours.

MACARONI SNOW PUDDING.—Take three ounces macaroni, one pint of new milk, one gill of cream, four of brown sugar or molasses, and eight tablespoonfuls of snow. Simmer the macaroni in the milk till well mixed; add the sugar and cream; then stir in the snow quickly and bake immediately till slightly browned.

RICE AND APPLE PUDDING.—Boil half a pound of rice in half a pint of milk till it is soft; then fill the pudding dish half full of apples, which have been pared and cored; sweeten with brown sugar or molasses; put the rice over the fruit as a crust, and bake one hour.

SNOW BALL PUDDING.—Pare and core large mellow apples, and inclose them in cloths spread over with boiled rice, and boil one hour. Dip them in cold water before turning them out. They may be eaten with syrup, sugar or sweetened milk.

FARINA PUDDING.—Mix ten ounces of farina with half a pint of cold milk; put one quart of milk over the fire, and while it is boiling stir in the farina gradually, and let it simmer fifteen or twenty minutes. It may be served with milk, fruit, jelly or sugar.

FIG AND COCOANUT PUDDING.—Wash one pound of figs in warm water; soak them till soft; add to them one grated cocoanut with its milk, and four ounces of sugar; then knead with them all as much wheat meal as can be worked into a rather soft dough. (If in the cold season, three or four spoonfuls of snow will make it lighter.) Tie it in a pudding bag, not very tight, as it will swell some; and boil two hours.

APPLE PUDDING.—Boil one pound and a half of good apples with a gill of water and half a pound of brown sugar, till reduced to a smooth pulp; stir in one gill of sweet cream, a tablespoonful of flour or fine bread crumbs; flavor with a little lemon juice or grated lemon, and bake forty minutes.

POTATO APPLE DUMPLINGS.—Boil any quantity of white mealy potatoes; pare, and mash them with a rolling pin; then dredge in flour enough to form a dough; roll it out to about the thickness of pie crust, and make up the dumplings by putting an apple, pared, cored, and quartered, to each. Boil or bake one hour.

NOTE.—If the crust be made in the same manner as for cream pie crust, these are very nice.

GREEN CORN PUDDING.—To one quart of grated ears of sweet corn, add a teacupful of cream, one gill of milk, a tablespoonful of flour, and two ounces of sugar; mix all together and bake an hour and a half.

THE FRUITS.

WE come now to one of the most important departments of dietetics, viz.: fruit, and the necessity of its culture, preservation, and use. Next to good bread, there is nothing that can compare in value as an article of diet with good ripe fruit. People have been accustomed to consider fruit more in the light of a relish and a luxury, rather than as what it really should be—a staple article of diet, and a necessity of every meal.

Would people place their bread and fruit as the central dishes of their tables, around which other dishes are grouped as convenience or taste may dictate, instead of as now placing the meat as the staple article, what a vast amount of labor, sickness, and suffering would be avoided!

Good unleavened bread and the variety of fruits in their season contain all the elements necessary to the support of human life. And while there is a large class of vegetables, which are nutritious, palatable, and wholesome, making variety enough to suit the most fastidious, yet fruit must ever take the precedence as the BEST food for human beings.

But, say many, "fruit is so expensive, we can't afford it; besides, if all were to use fruit freely, there would not be half enough in the country to supply the markets." No fear on that score. Let the demand come, and the supply will soon follow. And as to not being "able to afford it," let us see. Suppose, good friends, you dispense entirely with your tobacco, tea, coffee, pork, nutmeg, pepper, and all manner of spices; your cakes, pickles, preserves, etc.; you would find your tables would cost you much less than they now do, and you would be infinitely the gainers, not only in health, strength, and happiness, but also in the pleasures of the table.

And until our farmers turn their attention more to fruit culture, which they can easily do if they choose; until they give it the place and importance which it deserves and demands, all attempts at dietetic reform will be for their wives an up-hill business; and will, in a majority of cases, only end at last in total failure. Now a good fruit garden is generally looked upon as a fine luxury—a thing very

(18)

desirable but not at all practicable.—a plot of ground to be planted and taken care of, if planted and cared for at all, at odd moments, or, else neglected entirely ; whereas, it should be considered a necessity, an inseparable adjunct of every farm, no more to be dispensed with or neglected than the corn crop or wheat field, And our farmers will find that the outlay of time and labor requisite to plant a fruit garden which shall soon yield an abundance of delicious fruit, will be much less than they have any idea of. And if they will but try the experiment of planting even two acres to strawberries, raspberries, Lawton blackberries, grapes, peaches, plums, pears, cherries, currants, gooseberries, etc., and devote the time, even, that they now spend in raising, feeding and butchering their hogs, (those measly, scrofulous abominations,) to · its cultivation and care, I think they will find themselves not only vastly the gainers in health and happiness, but that they will also have more toward supplying their families with good wholesome food from two acres, than from any ten devoted to stock raising.

Fruit should be used as far as possible in its natural state. Ripe, uncooked apples, pears, peaches, plums, grapes, strawberries, raspberries, etc., are incomparably superior in point of wholesomeness to the same fruits when cooked, and should, in their season, be upon the table at every meal. Many persons may object to this, especially during the summer months, saying that fruit is the cause of summer and bowel complaints, etc. That unripe fruit at any time, and even the best of ripe fruit eaten between meals, especially if meat forms a part of the daily food, often does induce these disorders I admit, but that only proves the truth of the old adage, "The greatest blessings become the greatest curses if wrongly applied." The same is true of fruit as of anything else. It should never under any circumstances be eaten between meals. The majority of the diarrheas, fevers, etc., so prevalent in summer, are owing chiefly to the heating, stimulating effects of the meat, spices, condiments, rich cake, pastry, etc., in common use. Very few cases of these diseases have ever been known to occur, where the principal part of the person's diet had been coarse bread, ripe fruit and good vegetables. And if those who regard a mixed diet as necessary, would, during the summer months, partake very sparingly of meat, substituting fruit mainly in its place, eating it as a part of, and only with their regular meals, and in proper quantities, they would find their doctor's fee sensibly diminished, and their own health vastly improved. As far as practicable, a supply of long-keeping fruits should be secured for the winter and early spring ; but at present it is hardly possible to preserve a quantity sufficient for the whole year, without some artificial means of preservation. As to the labor of canning fruit, it is much less than is generally supposed. All the smaller kinds, such as berries, cherries, peaches, etc., can be canned much more easily and expeditiously than they can be dried. I give below the plan recommended by the AMERICAN AGRICULTURIST, a paper, by the way, which no farmer's family can afford to do without.

PRESERVING FRUITS.

"For several years past we have been trying to abolish the old mode of preserving fruits, viz.: the addition of pound for pound of sugar, and stewing them down to an indigestible mass in order to make them ' keep.' Our efforts in this direction have been in a measure successful; the high price of sugar this year will do much toward the adoption of the newer and better mode. All kinds of fruits can be preserved for a year, or more, with the use of little or no sugar, and at the same time retain nearly all their natural flavor. The process is not more difficult, and is less costly than the stewing process, while the fruit is far more delicious and healthful. The whole operation depends upon simply heating the fruit through, and then keeping it entirely free from the access of air.

FRUIT JARS.

Periodically, as the fruit season approaches, there are numerous fruit jar inventions, patented and otherwise, brought before the public with wonderful assurance and an indefinite number of extravagant recommendations. Some seal with wax, others with India rubber and cast iron; in some the tops are screwed on; in others wedged; and in others wired. Some tin, some glass, and some stone, but *all* are " perfect," if the claims of the inventors and manufacturers are fully credited. We have tried most of these fruit jars, and while many of them are good, our experience has led us to adopt the cheapest kinds of glass bottles and jars. Tin cans are not safe. While in a majority of cases they may answer well for a season or two, there is always danger of their corrosion, or rusting, and the consequent production of poisonous salts of tin. Besides, it is desirable to have the fruit in transparent vessels so that it can always be examined. Good well-glazed stone-ware bottles and jars are not objectionable on account of corrosion, but they are opaque, so that the contents can not be seen, and are but little cheaper than cheap glass.

During the past year we have kept several bushels of fruit of different kinds, always in good condition, and the portion now unused is almost as fresh and delicious as when first picked. For keeping we have used all sorts of *glass* bottles and jars, holding from a pint to two quarts each —including several of the patent jars with caps of various patterns. Among these were a dozen glass jars with India rubber rings expanded by a compressing screw, of which five gave way and the

FIG. 1.

fruit was lost. Of the common glass bottles and jars we have not lost one. There is hardly a glass bottle of whatever form that cannot be turned to account for preserving fruits—even junk bottles, soda-water bottles, jars, &c., &c. The *best* form is a wide-mouthed quart bottle or jar, the neck drawn in to give a shoulder for the cork to rest upon.

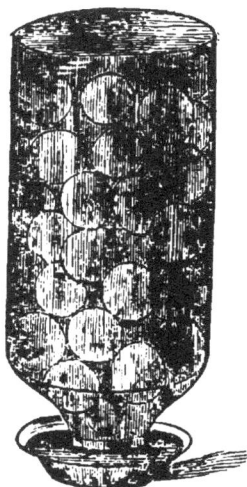

Fig. 2.   Fig. 3.

For the larger fruits wide necks are needed; for the smaller berry fruits, narrow necks answer perfectly.

PREPARING THE FRUIT.

Our method is, to put the fruit in a preserving kettle of some kind —a glazed iron kettle, or even a tinned one, or a tin pail will do— and sweeten it with just sugar enough to fit it for the table. The sweetening is added in the form of a syrup made by boiling from one to three pounds of sugar (usually 2 lbs.) with one quart of water. The more juicy fruits, such as strawberries, require less syrup, while pears and quinces require more. The fruit is heated with the syrup just long enough to scald it *through*. Some prefer to use less sweetening and add more when the fruit is to be used. Others use no sugar; they think the fruit keeps just as well, and preserves its aroma better without any sugar. We prefer to use all the sugar that is to be needed, believing that the fruit will probably keep more certainly, and it is then always ready to pour out at once upon the table. The fruit to be preserved should be in good condition—ripe, but not over-ripe, nor containing any decayed portions. Tomatoes are peeled, and then cooked down one-half, as this makes a better sauce, and requires less bottle room.

BOTTLING THE FRUIT.

The bottles or jars are thoroughly cleansed, and each one fitted with a stopper. For these, soft corks are best; but they may be made of soft dry wood. For each bottle or jar we provide a little tin "patty-pan," (fig. 1,) costing one-half to one cent each by the quantity. Tea-saucers will answer. For *cement* we heat together in an old tin basin or iron kettle, one pound of rosin, and one and one-half to two ounces of tallow. This may be mixed in quantity, and melted from time to time as wanted. We formerly used a little over one ounce of tallow to one pound of rosin, but further experience is in favor of a softer cement, when the fruit is to stand in a cool cellar. While the fruit is being heated, as above described, the bottles are well warmed by setting them near the fire and frequently turning them; or better, by setting them in cold water in a wash-boiler and heating to the boiling point. The fruit being barely scalded *through*, it is dipped hot into the heated bottles, through a funnel, if the bottle necks are small. This is done carefully, so as not to mash the fruit. The bottles are filled up to where the bottom of the stoppers will come; they are then jarred a little to make the air bubbles rise, and more fruit or syrup added if needed. The tops and necks are then wiped clean, inside and out and the stoppers put in, and sunk to a level with the top. The cement being warmed in the mean time, a little is dipped on over the stoppers to close them tightly. The bottles are then turned necks down in the little patty-pans, or saucers, (fig. 2,) and a quantity of cement dropped in to completely enclose the stoppers and necks. When cold the bottles may be set either side up (fig. 2 or 3). The cooling will shrink the contents so as to create a strong inward pressure, but the patty-pans prevent the stoppers from being pressed in, and the cement shuts out the air.

The whole process is simple and quickly performed. After the fruit is prepared, two persons will heat it, and put up 50 to 100 bottles in half a day. We prefer quart bottles, as these furnish enough for once opening. If cork stoppers are used, they are rendered soft and pliable, and may be crowded into a small orifice, by first soaking them in hot water.

SUBSTITUTE FOR PATTY-PANS.

The patty-pans are simply circular pieces of tin, stamped in the form of a cup or plate, two to three and one-half inches across. We buy them at wholesale for 87 cts., or $1.25 per gross. But any kind of cup to hold the wax, will answer. We have seen the common blacking boxes used, bottom for one jar or bottle, and the top or cover for another. Blocks of wood, or bits of board, cut out into cup-form with a gouge, or bored only part way through with a large auger, answer every purpose. They should be partly filled with cement, before turning the bottle into them. No one need look far for the materials. The old bottles about the house, thoroughly cleaned, the tin boxes, or old saucers, or wooden blocks, and some rosin are all the apparatus needed. "

FIG. 4.

The above method is good, but the following is still better, being safer, surer, more simple and less expensive. Out of hundreds of quarts which last year were put up in this manner for the Hygienic Institute, not one has been lost, and we have them now, in July, as perfect as the hour they were canned. No corks are used; the cloths will answer a second year, and as soon as the bottles are cold it can be ascertained with absolute certainty whether they are air-tight or not. The following is

OUR METHOD.—Take common, wide-mouthed glass bottles or jars ; those with a rim around the neck are preferable. Procure thick Canton flannel ; cut it into squares sufficiently large to cover the top and neck of the jar. Dip these pieces into heated grafting wax made by melting together one pound rosin, two ounces beeswax and one and one-half ounces tallow. Several pieces may be put in at one time, and should be allowed to remain in until they are perfectly saturated with the wax. Just before filling a jar with fruit, take out one of these pieces, thus allowing it to cool a little. By doing so they can be handled with greater ease and there is no danger of the wax running through them into the fruit. After the wax has been kept hot a long time it is apt to harden slightly. A little tallow should then be added.

In preparing the fruit, one pound of sugar to six pounds of raspberries, wild blackberries, whortleberries, etc., is sufficient—while for Lawton blackberries, strawberries, and the more acid fruits, one pound to four is requisite. Add a small quantity of water and cook the fruit a trifle less than if it were to be used immediately upon the table.

Heat the bottles to prevent breaking ; this may be done by placing them underneath the stove, or else by putting them into a kettle of cold water and gradually heating it. Pour the HOT fruit into the HOT bottle, filling it full ; wipe the top and outside of the neck of the bottle PERFECTLY DRY ; have ready a piece of white paper cut so that it will just fit the INSIDE of the mouth of the bottle, and lay it on the top of the fruit Now you are prepared for the sealing process. The pieces of Canton flannel being all ready, having been previously saturated with the wax and allowed to cool three or four minutes, place one of them over the mouth of the bottle, drawing it as tightly as possible, and then wind a piece of strong twine round and round, binding the edges of the cloth firmly against the neck of the bottle. Then with a spoon dip on a little of the hot wax spreading it evenly over the top of the cloth, and over this place a paper large enough to cover the top and neck of the bottle, smoothing it as closely as possible, and the jar is sealed. As soon as the bottles cool, a glance will determine whether they are air-tight or not, as, if so, there will be a slight depression of the cover. The least hole "will prevent this concavity, and thus indicate at once the necessity of repeating the sealing process." If care be taken, not one bottle in forty will fail of being perfectly sealed at first.

In a very large family, glazed stone jugs, holding from one to two gallons, may be used. In this case the handles of the jugs will interfere with the tying of the cloths, and corks will therefore have to be substituted in place of them. Immerse the corks in hot water till thoroughly soaked, (they should be from one inch and a half to two inches in length, and should fit the jug so tightly that previous to soaking it will be very difficult to drive them in)—fill the jug with fruit, then with a hammer or mallet drive the cork in tightly till the top of it is just level with the mouth of the jug. Dip on plenty of the hot wax, covering the whole top completely. When cold, set them away in a cool, dry place, and they will keep for years as fresh as when first put up.

In order to save various kinds of fruits and ensure variety, next to canning, the best method is that of drying, and for the larger fruits, such as apples, etc., the latter is much the cheaper and more practicable method.

The essential requisites in drying fruit are : First, that it should dry quickly, so as to preserve as far as possible its natural flavor. Second, that it should dry thoroughly in order to keep well; and third, that it should be kept free from dust and flies.

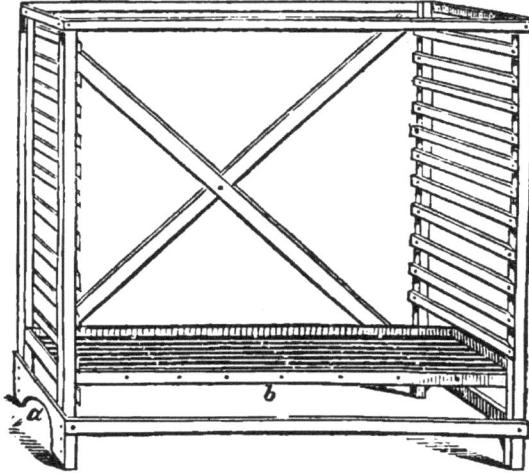

The accompanying engraving represents it; (*b*) is a rack four feet long and about one and one-half feet wide, made of common wall lath nailed together one-tenth to one-fourth of an inch apart, according to the size of the fruit to be dried. A lath or strip of board one inch wide is nailed round the edge to prevent the fruit's falling off. The whole expense is but a mere trifle. Any person who can drive nails can make it. If laths are not to be had, strips of boards will do as well.

Now for a place to keep them in the house conveniently, that the fruit will continue to dry during nights and stormy days. To effect this we constructed a frame represented in the engraving. Posts two inches square with strips about one inch square nailed across, far enough apart to admit a rack between them, and braced as represented in the cut. A frame to hold twenty racks can be made for a dollar, and not weigh over twenty pounds. This we set near the kitchen stove against the wall, out of the way and occupying the space of a good sized bureau, having over one hundred square feet surface of drying racks holding four or five bushels of apples or other fruit.

Our experience in the use of dried fruit is that the quicker it is dried the better it retains its flavor. Keeping off flies, wasps, &c., for cleanliness is of great importance. A few yards of musquito bars is sufficient to cover a large surface and prevent drying very little.

RECIPES FOR COOKING FRUIT.

BAKED APPLES.—The best baking apples are moderately tart, or very juicy, sweet ones. The former, of ordinary size, will bake in about thirty minutes; the latter in about forty-five minutes. Select, for baking, apples of nearly equal size; wipe them dry and clean; put a very little water in the bottom of the baking vessel, and place them in a hot oven.

STEWED GREEN APPLES.—Apples for stewing should be well flavored and juicy. Sweet apples, when stewed, turn more or less dark colored, and hence do not appear as well as tart ones at the table, though some persons prefer them. Pare, core, and quarter; put a little water to them, and boil moderately till soft, and add sufficient sugar to suit taste—more or less, according to the acidity of the fruit. Some cooks flavor them with lemon; others with a small portion of peaches or other fruit. Good apples, however, are good enough in and of themselves.

BOILED APPLES.—Select round, mellow apples of uniform size; pare them; boil in as little water as possible, till soft; put them in a vegetable dish; and slowly pour over them a syrup, made by dissolving half a pound of sugar in a pint of boiling water.

STEWED PIPPINS.—A rich apple sauce is made as follows: Peel, core, and quarter half a dozen ribstone pippins; put them into a pan with six ounces of brown sugar, the juice of a lemon, its thin rind cut into strips, and very little water; stew over a very slow fire till quite tender.

PEARS.—Pears may be baked, boiled, or stewed in the same manner as apples. Some varieties of small, early, and sweet pears are very delicious, boiled whole without paring, and sweetened with syrup. The large pears are usually selected for baking.

BOILED PEACHES.—They should be pared—except when the skins are very smooth, clean, and tender—but not stoned; boiled moderately till sufficiently cooked, and then sweetened.

STEWED DRIED PEACHES.—Most of the dried peaches in our markets are sour and unpleasant. But when we can find them of good quality, they are very excellent stewed and sweetened, precisely like dried apples.

UNCOOKED PEACHES.—When we have peaches as good and ripe as all peaches ought to be, the best way to prepare them is this: Peel them; cut the fruit off the stones in quarters, or smaller pieces; fill the dish; stir in a little sugar, and sprinkle a little more over the top

APRICOTS.—Ripe apricots may be prepared in the same way as peaches, but they are best with no preparation at all.

CHERRIES.—Stewing is the only proper method for cooking this fruit. Remove the stalks from the cherries; pick them over carefully, rejecting all unsound ones; put them into a pan, with a very little water, and sugar in the proportion of about three ounces to a pound of cherries; simmer them slowly over the fire, shaking the pan round occasionally till done. If a richer article is wanted, take the cherries out with a colander spoon, and keep them in a basin till cold; reduce the sweetened water to the consistency of syrup, and put it over the cherries.

QUINCES.—It has been said that quinces commend themselves more to the sense of smell than taste; hence are better to "adorn" other preparations than to be prepared themselves. When stewed till quite tender, and sweetened, they are, however, a very pleasant, yet rather expensive kind of sauce. In the form of marmalade, they are a better seasoning for bread, cakes, or puddings, than butter.

QUINCE MARMALADE.—Pare, core, and quarter the quinces; boil them gently, uncovered, in water, till they begin to soften; then strain them through a hair sieve, and beat, in a mortar or wooden bowl, to a pulp; add to each pound of fruit three quarters of a pound of sugar; boil till it becomes stiff, and pour into small molds or sweetmeat pots.

STEWED CRANBERRIES.—Wash and pick the berries; stew them in just as little water as will prevent their burning, till they become soft; then add half a pound of sugar to a pound of the fruit, and simmer a few minutes.

BLACKBERRIES.—When very ripe and sweet, a little sugar dusted over them is a sufficient preparation for the table. If sour, or not quite ripe, they should be stewed till soft, and moderately sweetened. The same rules apply to all berried fruits for which recipes are not given.

WHORTLEBERRIES.—Many prefer these uncooked and unseasoned. If stewed, however, they require but very little sweetening.

RASPBERRIES.—Red raspberries are never fit to be eaten till ripe, and then they require neither sugar nor cooking. Black raspberries, when quite ripe, are also best in a "state of nature." If not entirely ripe, they may be stewed a few minutes, and sweetened with a very little sugar or molasses.

CURRANTS.—Green currants, when half or two-thirds grown, are more mild flavored and pleasant than when fully ripe; nor do I find them often disagreeing with ordinary dyspeptics. They require stewing but a short time, and moderately sweetening. The best currants, when quite ripe, may be eaten uncooked, with a sprinkling of sugar.

PLUMS.— These must be managed according to their character and flavor. Many varieties are too sour to be eaten without stewing, and the addition of considerable sugar. Some kinds, however, are sweet and luscious enough to require neither.

GRAPES.—Good, ripe, well-cultivated Delawares, Isabellas, and Catawbas are incomparably superior in dietetic character, without "the interference of art." What a blessing it would be to the human race if all the vineyards in the world were made to supply wholesome food for children, instead of pernicious poison for adults!

PINEAPPLE.—The only way of preparing this fruit, which, like some others, has more flavor than taste, is that of paring, slicing, and sprinkling with sugar.

TOMATOES.—Scald the tomatoes by pouring boiling water on them; peel off the skins; then stew them for an hour, and add a little slightly toasted bread. This is an excellent sauce for Hygienic tables; and the fruit may be improved in flavor by stewing half an hour, or even an hour longer.

BOILED APPLES.—Select rich, fair, sweet apples of uniform size—the Tallman Sweeting is the best for this purpose. Leave the skins on them, merely removing the blossom ends with a sharp pointed knife. Wash them thoroughly, place them in a porcelain kettle and sprinkle over them a small quantity of sugar. Then add boiling water barely sufficient to cover them and cook slowly till tender.

PRUNES.—Prunes should be thoroughly washed, then soaked in just water enough to cover them, for an hour or two before cooking. Add sugar sufficient to sweeten them, and stew slowly till tender.

CIDER APPLE SAUCE.—Take six quarts sweet apples quartered and cored, pour over them one and one-half pints boiling water, and cook slowly. When about one third done add one-half cup sugar and three-fourths of a pint of boiled cider or apple syrup, and cook till they can be pierced easily with a fork.

NOTE.—These proportions make a much better sauce than where *more* boiled cider is used. We wish this dish might be brought into more general use. If properly cooked it is excellent. Every one in the country knows how boiled cider is made, but every one in the city is not supposed to, from the fact that it is a commodity rarely met with in the city markets. It is made by taking new, sweet cider fresh from the press, and boiling it down till it is about the consistency of common molasses. It is more wholesome than sugar, and added to apples in this way it is much more palatable.

STRAWBERRIES.—Cooking deteriorates strawberries more than any other kind of fruit. If cooked at all they should be simply sweetened and stewed.

STEWED DRIED APPLES.—Select rich, mellow, flavored fruits, which are clear from dark spots or mould. Wash and pick the pieces, boil in just water enough to cover them over a slow fire, till partially softened; then add sugar or molasses and continue the boiling till done.

DRIED GRAPES.—Dried grapes and dried apples, in the proportion of one-third of the former to two-thirds of the latter, make excellent sauce for the spring months.
Any kind of dried fruit, cherries, raspberries, peaches, quinces, &c., may be cooked with dried apples, and form quite a pleasing variety.

WHORTLEBERRY CRACKER SAUCE.—Stew whortleberries till quite soft, making them a little sweeter and more juicy than usual. As soon as they are done cover the bottom of a porcelain kettle or strong stone jar with a layer of Dr. Trall's crackers, and cover them completely with the sauce, then add another layer of crackers, then more sauce, and so on till you have as much as you wish. Let them soak over night, and you have a very fine dish for breakfast. It should be as juicy as common sauce when ready for the table, therefore it is necessary to add much more water than usual to the berries, when cooking.
Apple sauce prepared in this way is esteemed very nice by many.

VEGETABLES.

BOILED POTATOES.—Wash the potatoes without cutting them; put them in boiling water, with not more of water than is sufficient to cover them; boil moderately until they are softened so that a fork will readily penetrate them; pour off the water and let them stand till dry. Young potatoes of medium size will cook in about twenty-five minutes; old potatoes require double that time. When peeled they will cook in about half the time. All who would have potatoes well cooked must observe the following particulars: Always take them out of the water the moment they are done. Ascertain when they are done, by pricking with a fork, and not leave them to crack open. When cooked in any way, they become heavy and "watery" by cooking them after they are once softened through. They should be selected of an equal size, or the smallest should be taken up as fast as cooked. Potatoes should never be boiled *very* hard, as it is apt to break them; nor should the water stop boiling, as it will tend to make them "watery." Old potatoes are improved by soaking in cold water several hours or over night, before cooking. They should never remain covered after having been roasted or boiled, to keep them hot.

MASHED POTATOES.—Pare and wash the potatoes; drop them into water which is boiling very hard; let them boil moderately till done. As soon as they will pierce easily with a fork, pour off the water, place them over the fire again for a couple of minutes till perfectly dry, then mash them till they are entirely free from lumps. If any seasoning is desired, a little rich milk or sweet cream is all that is sufficient.

BROWNED MASHED POTATOES.—Prepare the same as mashed potatoes above; turn them immediately into a deep platter or dripping pan, smooth them evenly and place in a hot oven till browned.

POTATO BALLS.—Take mashed potatoes, either cold or hot, and form them into small round cakes of three-fourths of an inch in thickness. Place them in a hot oven, and let them remain till well browned.

STEWED POTATOES.—Cut cold boiled potatoes into thin slices, cover with milk or diluted sweet cream, and stew slowly till warmed through.

CHOPPED POTATOES.—Place cold boiled potatoes in a wooden bowl; chop them with a chopping knife till very fine; turn them into a deep platter; add milk till they are nearly covered, and bake in a moderately hot oven half an hour; stir them occasionally at first, then let a nice brown crust form upon them.

BROWNED POTATOES.—Cut cold boiled potatoes into slices one-third of an inch in thickness; lay them on a platter in a hot oven till both sides are moderately browned.

(28)

BROWNED POTATOES.—Boil potatoes of a nearly uniform size till about two-thirds done; pour off the water; remove the skins; place them in a hot oven, and bake till done. When baked potatoes are wanted in haste, this is a very quick and excellent method.

BREAKFAST POTATOES.—Pare and wash the potatoes. Cut them in pieces one-third of an inch in thickness; boil in as little water as possible, so that it will nearly all be evaporated in cooling. When done, add a small quantity of sweet cream or milk thickened with a little flour.

SWEET POTATOES.—These may be baked with their skins on, or peeled and boiled, and then browned a little in the oven, or simply boiled with or without the skins. They are excellent sliced and browned the next day after having been boiled, or even laid in the oven and browned.

MASHED PARSNEPS.—Wash them thoroughly, and remove the skins by scraping. Split them in halves or quarters, and boil till tender. When done, mash them the same as potatoes.

BROWNED PARSNEPS.—Cold parsneps may be cut in pieces one-half inch in thickness and browned in the oven the same as potatoes. They are nice for breakfast.

STEWED PARSNEPS.—Wash, scrape, and cut the parsneps into thin slices. Stir them in just water enough to prevent their burning. When nearly cooked, add a little boiling milk, and thicken with a small quantity of flour wet with cold milk. Let them simmer fifteen minutes.

CARROTS.—Carrots may be boiled, stewed, or browned in the same manner as parsneps. When stewed they are a favorite dish with many persons.

BOILED TURNIPS.—When turnips are sweet and tender, they are best if boiled whole till soft, and then sent immediately to the table. If they are allowed to boil too long they become bitterish. An hour is the medium time. They are less watery and better flavored when boiled with their skins on, and pared afterward.

MASHED TURNIPS.—This is the best method of preparing watery turnips and a good way of cooking all cookable kinds. Pare, wash, and cut them in slices; put them in just enough boiling water to cover them; let them boil till soft; pour them into a seive or colander and press out the water; mash them with fresh milk or sweet cream until entirely free from lumps; then put them into a saucepan over the fire, and stir them about three minutes.

BOILED CABBAGE.—Take off the outer leaves; cut the head in halves or quarters, and boil quickly in a large quantity of water till done; then drain and press out the water, and chop fine. Cabbage requires boiling from half an hour to an hour.

STEWED CABBAGE.—Slice the cabbage very fine, pour over it boiling water, nearly sufficient to cover it. Let it cook quickly till tender. Add boiling milk and thicken with flour wet with cold milk. Let it simmer fifteen minutes. This is excellent.

CAULIFLOWER.—Cut off the green leaves; plunge the heads in boiling water and let them cook from twenty minutes to half an hour. Split the heads open and lay them in halves in vegetable dishes, and cover with a sauce made with boiling milk, thickened with flour wet with cold milk, and boiled till well cooked.

GREENS.—Spinach, beet tops, cabbage-sprouts, mustard leaves, turnip leaves, cowslips, dandelions, and deerweed are all excellent for greens. They all require to be carefully washed and cleaned. Spinach should be washed repeatedly.. All the cooking requisite is boiling till tender, and drain on a colander. Lemon juice is the only admissible seasoning.

BOILED BEET ROOT. — Wash the roots carefully; avoid scraping, cutting or breaking the roots, as the juice would escape and the flavor be injured; put them into a pan of boiling water; let them boil one or two hours according to size; then put them in cold water and rub off the skin with the hand, and cut them in neat slices of uniform size. Good beets are sweet enough intrinsically, and need no seasoning.

NOTE.—Beet root must not be probed with a fork, as are potatoes. When done, the thickest part will yield to the pressure of the fingers.

BAKED BEETS.—Wash the roots clean, and bake whole till quite tender; put them in cold water; rub off the skin; if large, cut them in round slices, but if small, slice them lengthwise. If any seasoning is insisted on, lemon juice is the most appropriate. When baked slowly and carefully, beet root is very rich, wholesome, and nutritious. It usually requires baking four or five hours.

STEWED BEETS.—Take baked or boiled beet root, pare and cut it into thin slices; simmer in milk or diluted sweet cream fifteen minutes, and thicken the gravy with a little wheaten flour.

STRING BEANS.—When very young, the pods need only to be clipped, cut finely, and boiled till tender. When older, cut or break off the ends, strip off the strings that line their edges; cut or break each pod into three or four pieces, and boil. When made tender, a little cream or milk may be simmered with them a few minutes.

ASPARAGUS.—Put the stalks in cold water; cut off all that is very tough; tie them in bundles; put them over the fire and let them boil fifteen to twenty-five minutes, or until tender without being soft. No one has a right to desire a better vegetable than this with no other preparation than boiling. It should be cooked soon after being picked, or kept cool and moist in a cellar till wanted.

STEWED ASPARAGUS.—Cut the tender parts of the stalks into pieces of half an inch in length. Wash them; put them in enough boiling water to cook them without burning, and when nearly done add a small quantity of sweet cream or milk thickened with flour.

STEWED CUCUMBERS.—Pare and cut them into quarters, taking out the seeds; boil like asparagus; serve up with toasted bread and sweetcream.

VEGETABLE MARROW.—Peel the marrows; cut them in halves; scrape out the seeds; then boil about twenty minutes, or until soft; drain them, wash them, add a little milk or cream, and simmer a short time.

SALSIFY (OYSTER PLANT).—Scrape the vegetable; cut it in strips; parboil it; then chop it up with milk and a little sweet cream, and simmer gently till cooked very tender.

BROCCOLI.—Peel the stalks, and boil them fifteen minutes; tie the shoots into bunches; add a little milk or cream and stew gently for ten minutes.

WHOLE GRAINS AND SEEDS.

BOILED WHEAT.—Select fair, plump wheat; pick it over carefully and wash it perfectly clean. Let it soak in cold water twenty-four hours. Boil it in the same water (adding more if necessary) till perfectly soft. It will require several hours to cook it. It may be eaten with milk, or cream, or sugar, or without any of these, as preferred.

BOILED RICE.—Be careful and select for this purpose the large, plump kernel called *head-rice*; boil it in pure, soft water and in a covered vessel about twenty minutes, stirring it gently occasionally; then set it off from the fire, and in a place just warm enough to simmer; let it remain an hour and a half *without stirring*; the grains may then be taken out full and unbroken.

NOTE.—The *best* method of cooking rice is to cover it well with water and set it in a moderate oven, stirring it occasionally. When nearly done and the water mostly absorbed, milk or sweet cream may be added if desired, making a very rich dish. Or the water may be omitted and it may be cooked entirely in milk, using the same proportions of milk and rice as for a pudding, but omitting the sugar.

Another excellent method of cooking rice is by steaming it. A double boiler, commonly called a "Farina Boiler," is best for this purpose, but if none can be had a tightly covered tin pan, set over a kettle of boiling water, will answer.

RICE AND APPLE.—When the rice is about one-third cooked add a small quantity of tart apples sliced. When done, stir thoroughly together. If cooked in steam, this is a very nice dish.

RICE AND RAISINS.—An excellent dessert is made by adding one cup of raisins to three cups of rice and cooking in the ordinary manner, either in water or in equal parts of water and milk; or, if cooked by steam, it is delicious if cooked entirely in milk. To be eaten with sweetened cream or a sauce made by thickening boiling milk with corn starch and adding sugar to suit the taste.

BARLEY.—The common white or pearl barley is excellent, if cooked in the same manner as boiled wheat. Milk may be added when nearly done, if desired. It does not require cooking so long as the wheat.

PARCHED CORN.—Procure a wire apparatus called a "*corn popper.*" They can be bought at almost any hardware store for a mere trifle. The common "Tucket" corn is best for popping. Have the corn thoroughly dry. Place a large spoonful in the "popper," and pass it back and forth very quickly across the top of a *red hot* stove till done. Two minutes will suffice to produce a quart of great white kernels, as delicious as ever were eaten.

(31)

BOILED CHESTNUTS.—Boiled chestnuts, if made a part of our regular meals, are not only very delicious but perfectly wholesome. They should be first picked over very carefully and washed, then boiled from an hour to an hour and a half.

DRIED BEANS.—Pick the beans over carefully, wash them perfectly clean, cover them about three inches deep with cold water, and let them soak all night. Early in the morning place them over the fire, leaving upon them all the water that may remain unabsorbed and adding enough more to cook them in. Let them *simmer* slowly all the forenoon, but do not allow them to *boil*. When done, if any seasoning is desired a little sweet cream is sufficient. To bake them, take them from the fire about an hour before they are done, place them immediately in a deep pan, and bake one hour in a very hot oven.

NOTE.—Those who will try this method will be surprised to find how much superior it is to the ordinary way of cooking them.

DRIED PEAS—Are cooked precisely in the same manner as beans.

BOILED GREEN PEAS.—Washing green peas seems to extract much of their sweetness. If care be taken in shelling them they will not need washing. Immediately after shelling them put in boiling water sufficient to cover them, and boil from twenty to thirty minutes. When the pods are fresh and green, if they are washed and boiled in as little water as will cover them for fifteen or twenty minutes, and the juice added to the peas, it will improve the flavor. Sweet milk or cream is the only admissible seasoning.

BOILED GREEN BEANS.—The common garden, kidney, and Lima beans are all excellent dishes prepared by simply boiling till soft without destroying the shape of the seed. A little milk or cream may be stirred in, when they are cooked sufficiently, if any seasoning is desired. They usually require boiling an hour and a half.

BOILED GREEN CORN.—The only corn fit for boiling green is the sweet or evergreen corn. It should be simply husked, the silk removed and the ears plunged into boiling water and boiled from one-half to three-quarters of an hour.

STEWED CORN.—Cut the corn from the cob, boil it in just water enough to prevent burning. When done, add a little rich milk or sweet cream and a trifle of sugar.

SUCCOTASH.—The best materials for succotash are sweet corn and Lima beans. Cut the corn from the cobs, and when the beans have been cooking about three quarters of an hour add it to them, letting it cook about three-quarters of an hour longer. This is a dish "fit for a king." If any one desires a richer article, a little sweet cream may be added.

GREEN corn cut from the cob, green peas, green beans, (both Lima and common,) string beans, etc., may be canned by first thoroughly cooking in just water enough to cover them; then sealing in *tin* cans.

Green peas, beans, etc., may also ·be dried by first dropping them into boiling water, and letting them boil for two or three minutes, then draining and placing them where they will dry *quickly*. They are very nice when preserved in this way. I have eaten dried peas in June that I could not believe were not fresh from the garden, until I had been repeatedly assured that such was not the case; and when canned they are even nicer than when dried.

Tomatoes are canned by scalding, peeling, and cooking them as for the table; then putting up and sealing in the same manner as fruit cans are sealed. The secret of success in canning tomatoes is to *keep them boiling* from the time they begin to bubble up till put in the can. If allowed to cook awhile and then to partially stop boiling, or if cooked too long, they are apt to have a slightly bitter taste. If not cooked enough they will not keep well; but if pared, put immediately over the fire, and the boiling continued for a full hour after it begins, then put up immediately, they may be canned without the slightest difficulty; and will not only keep perfectly, but will be just as sweet and fresh as when first picked from the vines. If persons living in the country, who have the fresh materials for these things so profusely scattered around them, could but realize how delicious a dish of tomatoes, green peas, or succotash tastes in January or May, I think they would take much more pains than they now do to have their tables supplied with them.

GRUELS AND SOUPS.

WHEAT-MEAL GRUEL. — Mix two tablespoonfuls of wheat-meal smoothly with a gill of cold water; stir the mixture into a quart of boiling water; boil about fifteen minutes, taking off whatever scum forms on the top. A little sugar may be added if desired.

INDIAN-MEAL GRUEL.—Stir gradually into a quart of boiling water two tablespoonfuls of Indian-meal; boil it slowly twenty minutes. This is often prepared for the sick, under the name of "water-gruel." In the current cook-books, salt, sugar, and nutmeg are generally added. Nothing of the sort should be used, except sugar.

OATMEAL GRUEL.—Mix a tablespoonful of oatmeal with a little cold water; pour on the mixture a quart of boiling water, stirring it well; let it settle two or three minutes; then pour it into the pan carefully, leaving the coarser part of the meal at the bottom of the vessel; set it on the fire and stir it till it boils; then let it boil about five minutes, and skim.

FARINA GRUEL.—Mix two tablespoonfuls of farina in a gill of water; pour very gradually on the mixture a quart of boiling water, stirring thoroughly, and boil ten minutes.

TAPIOCA GRUEL.—Wash a tablespoonful of tapioca, and soak it in a pint and a half of water twenty minutes; then boil gently, stirring frequently, till the tapioca is sufficiently cooked, and sweeten.

SAGO GRUEL.—Wash two tablespoonfuls of sago, and soak it a few minutes in half a pint of cold water; then boil a pint and a half of water, and, while boiling, stir in the sago; boil slowly till well done, and sweeten with sugar or molasses.

CURRANT GRUEL.—Add two tablespoonfuls of currants to a quart of wheat-meal or oatmeal ground, and, after boiling a few minutes, add a little sugar.

GROAT GRUEL.—Steep clean groats in water for several hours; boil them in pure soft water till quite tender and thick; then add boiling water sufficient to reduce to the consistency of gruel. Currants and sugar may also be added.

ARROW-ROOT GRUEL.—Mix an ounce of arrow-root smoothly with a little cold water; then pour on the mixture a pint of boiling water, stirring it constantly; return it into the pan, and let it boil five minutes. Season with sugar and lemon-juice.

(34)

RICE GRUEL.—Boil two ounces of good clean rice in a quart of water until the grains are quite soft; then add two tablespoonfuls of sugar, and boil two or three minutes. Currants make a good addition to this gruel.

TOMATO SOUP.—Scald and peel good ripe tomatoes; stew them one hour, and strain through a coarse sieve; stir in a very little wheaten flour to give it body, and brown sugar in the proportion of a teaspoonful to a quart of soup; then boil five minutes. This is one of the most agreeable and wholesome of the "fancy dishes." Ochre, or gumbo, is a good addition to this and many other kinds of soup.

RICE SOUP.—Boil one gill of rice in a pint of water till soft; then add a pint of milk, a teaspoonful of sugar, and simmer gently five minutes.

SPLIT PEAS SOUP.—Soak the peas all night; then cook them three or four hours, or till perfectly soft. Add a little sweet cream just before they are done.

GREEN PEAS SOUP.—Take three pints of peas, three common sized turnips, one carrot, and the shells of the peas. Boil one quart of the largest of the peas, with the shells or the pods, till quite soft; rub through a fine colander; return the pulp into the pan, add the turnips, a carrot, sliced, and a quart of boiling water; when the vegetables are perfectly soft, add the young or smaller peas, previously boiled.

SPLIT PEAS AND BARLEY SOUP.—Take three pints of split peas, half a pint of pearl barley, half a pound of stale bread, and one turnip, sliced. Wash the peas and barley, and steep them in fresh water at least twelve hours; place them over the fire; add the bread, turnip, and half a tablespoonful of sugar; boil till all are quite soft; rub them through a fine colander, adding gradually a quart of boiling water; return the soup into the pan, and boil ten minutes.

BARLEY SOUP.—Take four ounces of barley, two ounces of bread crumbs, and half an ounce of chopped parsley. Wash the barley, and steep it twelve hours in half a pint of water; boil slowly in a covered tin-pan five hours, and about half an hour before the dish is to be served, add the parsley.

GREEN BEAN SOUP.—Take one quart of garden or kidney beans, one ounce of spinach, and one ounce of parsley. Boil the beans; skin and bruise them in a bowl till quite smooth; put them in a pan with two quarts of vegetable broth; dredge in a little flour; stir it on the fire till it boils, and put in the spinach and parsley, (previously boiled and rubbed through a sieve).

VEGETABLE BROTH.—This may be made with various combinations and proportions of vegetables. For example—four turnips, two carrots, one onion, and a spoonful of lentil flower. Half fill a pan with the vegetables, in pieces; nearly fill up the vessel with water; boil till all the vegetables are tender, and strain.

BARLEY BROTH.—Take four ounces of pearl barley, two turnips, three ounces of Indian-meal, and three ounces of sweet cream. Steep the pearl barley (after washing) twelve hours; set it on the fire in five quarts of fresh water, adding the turnips; boil gently an hour;

add the cream ; stir in the meal; thin it, if necessary, with more water, and simmer gently twenty minutes.

SPINACH SOUP.—Take two quarts of spinach, half a pound of parsley, two carrots, two turnips, one root of celery, and two ounces of cream. Stew all the ingredients in a pint of water—a few lemon parings may be thrown in to flavor—till quite soft ; rub through a coarse sieve ; add a quart of hot water, and boil twenty minutes.

VEGETABLE SOUP.—Take two good sized turnips, one carrot, one parsnep, one sweet potato, two Irish potatoes, one onion, a little parsley chopped fine, and three tablespoonfuls of rice or pearl barley. Slice the vegetables very thin ; put them into two quarts boiling water ; let them cook three hours, then add the rice, and cook one hour longer.

MISCELLANEOUS RECIPES.

CREAM CAKE.—One pint sweet cream, one teacupful white sugar, one cup English currants, Graham flour for a thin batter. Bake in muffing rings, or in gem tins; filling the latter only half full.

This is very nice, and is a near approach to a *strictly* hygienic cake.

STEAMED BREAD.—Make mush as for the table—Graham, hominy, or corn meal mush as preferred. When cool, to one quart add one pint of hot, boiled potatoes mashed through a collander, half a cup of molasses, one tea-cup of boiling milk, and equal parts of Indian meal and Graham or rye flour sufficient to make a rather soft dough. Place it in a deep basin or pan; smooth it evenly over the top; cover it tightly and steam four hours.

RYE AND INDIAN BREAD.—Take one part rye-meal and two parts of Indian; pour boiling water over the Indian, and stir it till the whole is sufficiently wet to work in the rye without adding any more water, and then, when about milk warm, work in the rye-meal. Should the dough be too stiff, add as much warm, *but not hot*, water as may be necessary; bake in a round iron dish from three to five hours. This bread, when new, or a day or two old, may be sliced and toasted; it is very sweet and wholesome. The crust is apt to fall off; this may be wet in water and put into a stone jar with some moderately tart apples, peeled and sliced, nicely covering the apples with the crust; then add a little water, and cover the dish with a tightly fitting cover; set it on the stove till the apples are cooked, and then take the crust off into plates; sweeten the apples to suit the taste, and spread it over the crust. This is an excellent dish, if care has been taken to prevent burning the crust.

OATMEAL CAKE.—Mix fine oatmeal into a stiff dough with milk-warm water; roll it to the thinness almost of a wafer; bake on a griddle or iron plates placed over a slow fire for three or four minutes; then place it on edge before the fire to harden. This will be good for months, if kept in a dry place.

SNOW BREAD.—Put into a basin or pan fresh Indian-meal and two or three times its bulk of snow; stir thoroughly together and try a little of the mixture on a hot griddle; if too dry, add more snow; if too moist, add meal. When just right, pour it into a deep pan, rounding it up in the middle about two inches thick, and cook from twenty minutes to half an hour in a *hot* oven. This, if properly made, is very light and nice.

(37)

SNOW CAKE.—Mix a little corn-meal and pulverized sugar with the dry flour, and stir in the snow; bake in a *hot* oven till well browned.

WHORTLEBERRY JOURNEY CAKE.—Take one pint of whortleberries, one small teacupful sugar, one pint corn-meal, one tablespoonful of flour. Wet the whole with *boiling* water, and bake in small, round cakes in a *hot* oven twenty minutes.

POTATO SCONES.—Mash boiled potatoes till quite smooth, and knead with flour to the consistency of a light dough; roll it about half an inch thich; cut the scones in any form desired; prick them with a fork and bake on a griddle.

MILK TOAST.—This is made by scalding sweet milk and thickening it with a very little moistened flour or cornstarch. Let it boil well. Split open the gems or diamonds, or whatever bread you choose to use; toast them nicely; then place them in a dish for the table, and cover with the thickened gravy.

CREAM TOAST.—Toast the bread and turn over it, while hot, boiling sweet cream diluted with milk.

WHEAT- MEAL FRUIT BISCUITS.—Mix Graham flour with just enough of scalded figs—previously washed—to make an adherent dough by much kneading; roll or cut into biscuits half an inch thick and two or three inches square; bake in a quick oven.

CUSTARD WITHOUT EGGS.—Take one quart of sweet, new milk, four tablespoonfuls of flour, two tablespoonfuls of sugar. Boil the milk over a brisk fire, and, when boiling, stir in the flour (having been previously mixed with cold milk to prevent lumping). When thoroughly scalded, bake in a crust, or in cups.

RICE CUSTARD.—Boil two ounces of ground rice in a pint and a half of new milk; add four ounces of sugar, an ounce of grated cocoa-nut, four ounces of sweet cream, and bake in a slow oven.

RASPBERRY CUSTARD.—Boil one pint of cream; dissolve half a pound of sugar in three gills of raspberry juice; mix this with boiling cream; stir till the whole is quite thick, and serve in custard glasses.

APPLE CREAM.—Pare and boil good rich, baking apples till soft; rub the pulp through a hair sieve; add the sugar while warm; when cold, stir in a sufficient quantity of sweet cream, and serve cold.

PINEAPPLE ICE CREAM.—Mix three gills of pineapple syrup with one pint of cream; add the juice of a large lemon, and four ounces of sugar; pour into a mould; cover it with white paper; lay a piece of brown paper over to prevent any water getting in, and set it in the ice.

STRAWBERRY CREAM.—Mash the fruit gently; drain it on a sieve, strewing a little sugar on it; when well drained (without being pressed), add sugar and cream to the juice, and, if too thick, a little milk. Whisk it in a bowl, and, as the froth rises, lay it on a sieve; and when no more will rise, put the cream in a dish, and lay the froth upon it.

RASPBERRY ICE CREAM.—Mash one pound of raspberries; strain off the juice; mix it with the cream; add sugar as required; whisk it; then pour into glasses, and freeze.

Note.—The bucket used for freezing should be large enough to allow four or five inches of ice, broken in small pieces and mixed with salt, to be placed below and around the sides of the mold.

CHERRY JAM.—Take four pounds of Kentish cherries, one pound of fine sugar, and half a pint of red currant juice. Stone the fruit, and boil the whole together, rather quickly, till it becomes soft.

APPLE CHEESE.—Take two pounds of apples, pared and sliced; one pound of sugar; the juice and grated rind of a lemon, and a little water. Put them all into a pan; cover, and set it over the fire till the apples are reduced to a pulp, turning the pan occasionally; let it boil twenty minutes, stirring constantly, and pour it into small molds.

BAKED MILK.—Put the milk into a jar; tie white paper over it; let it remain in a moderately warm oven all night, and it will be of the consistency of thin gruel.

STRAWBERRY SHORT-CAKE.—Make a rather stiff batter of rich milk or thin, sweet cream, and Graham flour. Bake in a quick oven. When done, cut open and put the berries, previously sweetened and slightly mashed, on the under-crust, sprinkle a very little sugar over, and add the other crust. No one need desire a more palatable or healthful fruit cake. Raspberries, blackberries, whortleberries, currants, tomatoes, oranges, and all of the juicy fruits, make an excellent dish thus prepared.

SNOW BALLS.—Spread boiled rice over a cloth and lay on the rice, berries, cherries, tomatoes, or oranges. Then tie closely, and boil in water just long enough to cook the fruit. When done, serve with a little sugar, syrup, or sweet cream.

RICE CAKE.—Two cups sweet cream, two cups rice, one quart Graham flour, eight large potatoes, three cups white sugar; boil the rice, also the potatoes; sift the latter as soon as done through a colander, and mix with the other ingredients. Both rice and potatoes should be hot. Bake in gem tins, half full.

RICE PIES.—Boil two cups of rice in one quart of milk. When done, add four quarts boiling milk, and sugar to taste. Bake same as custard pie. This quantity will make six pies.

APPENDIX.

In the foregoing pages are given the principal recipes for strictly hygienic cookery, such as are used upon the *patients'* table of the Hygienic Institute. To accommodate, however, that large class of persons, who desire a diet comparatively plain, and yet dislike to dispense entirely with all kinds of seasonings, I subjoin the following. They are, a part of them, such as are used upon our *boarders'* table, and compared with the rich cakes and pastry in common use may be considered quite physiological.

FINE FLOUR GEMS.—Gems made of fine flour in the same manner as of Graham, the batter being rather stiffer, however, say about like ordinary bread sponge, and baked in the gem-tins, are as light, and far sweeter, than any soda biscuit, and by all who have ever tasted them are pronounced the most delicious bread that ever was eaten.

PUFFS.—One pint sweet milk, three eggs, twelve heaping tablespoonfuls of fine flour. Beat the eggs thoroughly, make a smooth paste of the flour and part of the milk, add the eggs and the remainder of the milk, and bake in the gem-tins in a quick oven.

CORN BREAD.—One quart sour milk, one quart corn meal, one egg, one teaspoonful soda, one heaping tablespoonful butter.

CORN BREAD No 2.—One pint sweet milk, one pint Graham flour, one pint corn meal, one tablespoonful sweet cream, one tablespoonful molasses, one-half teaspoonful cream tartar, one-fourth teaspoonful soda.

CORN BREAD No 3.—Take one pint sweet milk, a heaping iron spoonful of wheat flour, two large spoonfuls of Indian meal, one teaspoonful soda, two teaspoonfuls cream tartar; bake in pie tins. It should be no stiffer than will pour out in the pans easily.

CORN BREAD No 4.—One pint of corn meal, one quart milk; boil the milk and scald the meal thoroughly; beat up three eggs; thin your dough to a batter with cold milk; add a piece of butter half as large as an egg; put in your eggs, with a little salt, pour in shallow pans, and bake brown.

PIE CRUST.—Take equal parts of corn meal, Graham flour and white flour, mix thoroughly with butter in the ratio of one cup of butter to nine pies; wet with water.

PIE-PLANT OR RHUBARB PIE.—Peel and cut the rhubarb in small pieces; then pour boiling water upon it, and placing it where it will keep hot, let it stand twenty minutes; drain off the water, fill your crust and sweeten to taste.

PUMPKIN PIE.—Stew your pumpkin slowly and for a long time as this makes the flavor richer; strain nicely through a collander, mix (not very thin) with milk and add one egg for each two pies; sugar to taste. Squash prepared in a similar manner is preferable to pumpkin.

CUSTARD PIE.—Four eggs, a quart of milk, sugar to taste.

RICE PIE.—Wash nicely two cups of rice, boil it in milk, then add to it nine eggs, six quarts milk, and sugar to taste.

The above pies are much improved if the milk is boiled before using and poured hot upon the other ingredients, being at the same time well stirred.

STEAMED PUDDING.—Three cups sugar; one cup butter; twelve cups sour milk; two cups raisins; six eggs; three teaspoonfuls soda; flour sufficient for a thick batter. Steam five or six hours.

RICE PUDDING WITH FRUIT.—In a pint of new milk put two large spoonfuls rice well washed, then add two apples, pared and quartered or a few currants or raisins, simmer slowly till the rice is very soft, then add one egg beaten to bind it. Serve with cream and sugar.

RICE PUDDING.—One-half teacupful of rice, two eggs and a few raisins, to one quart of milk; sweeten to taste.

CREAM PUDDING.—Beat up the yolks of four eggs and whites of two; add a pint of cream, a spoonful of flour, and a little sugar; beat till smooth; bake it in buttered cups.

BOSTON APPLE PUDDING.—Peel and core a dozen and a half good apples; cut them small and put them in a stew pan with a little water; stew over a slow fire till soft, sweeten with moist sugar and pass it through a hair sieve; add the yolks of four eggs, and one white, and the juice of a lemon; beat well together; line the inside of a deep dish with paste, put in the pudding and bake half an hour.

SWEET APPLE PUDDING.—Pare and core the apples, chop them fine, and stir them into a batter made of sweet cream, eggs and flour—say three eggs to a quart of cream and flour enough to make it not very thick; stir well and bake on buttered tins or pudding dishes. This needs to bake two or three hours; serve with sweetened cream.

BATTER PUDDING.—Six ounces fine flour, and three eggs; beat well with a little milk, added by degrees until it is the thickness of cream— put it into a buttered dish and bake three-quarters of an hour; or if preferred put in a buttered and floured basin tied over with a cloth and boil one hour and a half.

RICE AND APPLE PUDDING.—Core as many apples as will nearly fill your dish; boil them in a light syrup—prepare rice with milk and sugar: put some of the rice in the dish; put in the apples and fill up the interstices with rice; bake it in the oven till it is a fine color.

BREAD PUDDING. No 1.—Unfermented brown bread, two ounces; milk, half a pint; sugar, a quarter of an ounce; one egg; cut the bread in slices and pour the milk over it boiling hot; let it stand till well soaked, then stir in the egg and sugar thoroughly beaten, and bake or steam for one hour.

No. 2.—Take light white bread and cut in thin slices—put into a pudding-shape any kind of preserve, then a slice of bread, and repeat until the mould is nearly full; pour over all a pint of boiling milk in which two beaten eggs have been mixed; cover the mould with a piece of linen, place it in a sauce-pan with a little boiling water; let it boil twenty minutes; serve with pudding sauce.

CORN STARCH PUDDING.—One quart milk, four tablespoonfuls corn starch, two-thirds of a cup white sugar and a little lemon peel. Wet the corn starch with a little of the milk, boil the remainder of the milk with the sugar and lemon peel, add the starch and cook briskly three or four minutes. Turn out into cups or moulds. To be eaten with sweetened cream.

IMITATION CORN STARCH PUDDING.—Take one quart of milk, a little salt; boil two-thirds of the milk and thicken the other third with flour to quite a thick, smooth paste; add the yolks of two eggs well beaten and stir into the boiling milk—it will cook in a minute; have ready some cups previously wet in cold water, fill them to the required depth with the mixture; when cool enough to turn out without breaking, turn them bottom upwards on plates, place some jelly on the top, and prepare a sauce to suit the taste. The whites of the eggs with white sugar boiled in milk, and flavored to taste, is very nice.

HOMINY PORRIDGE.—Steep one pound of hominy in water ten hours, and then dry in a stove or oven; pour off the fluid which has not been absorbed; add three pints of milk, and set the whole in a moderate oven two hours, till all the milk is absorbed; pour into saucers, and serve with milk and sugar.

SAGO PORRIDGE.—Soak four tablespoonfuls of sago a few minutes in one quart of cold water; then boil it gently one hour, and pour it into soup plates.

RICE AND SAGO PORRIDGE.—Take equal quantities of rice flour or ground rice and sago, and proceed as for hominy porridge.

BEAN PORRIDGE.—Mix three tablespoonfuls of bean or lentil flour with one pint of water; boil ten minutes, stirring continually.

SODA BISCUIT.—One quart flour; two teaspoonfuls cream of tartar mixed well into the dry flour; one teaspoonful soda dissolved in sweet milk enough to make a soft dough with the flour. Bake in a quick oven.

BREAKFAST CAKES.—One quart flour; four eggs; a piece of butter the size of an egg; mix the butter well into the flour; beat the eggs light in a pint bowl and fill it up with cold milk; pour this gradually into the flour; work it for eight or ten minutes only, roll into thin cakes about the size of a breakfast plate, and bake in a quick oven.

CREAM SPONGE CAKE.—Two eggs, one cup white sugar, one-half cup cream; mix rather thin with Graham or white flour, and bake in gem tins.

SPONGE CAKE.—Four eggs, one cup sugar, one cup milk, one-fourth teaspoonful soda. Mix soft and bake.

JELLY CAKE.—Three eggs, one cup sugar; mix soft with Graham or fine flour, and bake very thin. Either of the last three recipes are nice for jelly cake, if baked thin.

SUGAR CAKE.—Three cups sugar, three cups sour milk, one cup butter, three eggs, sufficient soda to sweeten the milk.

MOLASSES CAKE. No. 1.—Three cups molasses, four cups sour milk, one-half cup butter, soda to sweeten the milk; mix rather stiff.

No. 2—One cup molasses, one-half cup butter, one teaspoonful soda dissolved in one-half cup warm water; mix of medium stiffness.

No. 3.—One-half cup molasses, one-half cup sugar, a piece of butter the size of an egg, one teaspoonful soda, one-half cup water; not stiff.

SILVER CAKE.-- One cup white sugar, one-half cup of butter, one and a half cups of flour, one teaspoonful of cream of tartar, one-half teaspoonful of soda, one teaspoonful extract of lemon.

GOLD CAKE.— One cup brown sugar, one-half cup of butter, the yolks of four eggs, one-half cup of sweet milk, one and a half cups of flour, one teaspoonful of cream of tartar, one-half teaspoonful of soda.

SPONGE CAKE.—One large coffee cup of sugar, one cup flour, five eggs. Beat yolks and sugar together, beat whites to a froth, mix all together, stirring as little as possible. Flavor with lemon juice or extract.

RAILROAD CAKE.—One cup sugar, one heaping cup flour, one teaspoonful cream tartar, one-half teaspoonful soda, three eggs and a little lemon juice. Stir all together ten minutes. Bake twenty minutes in a quick oven.

BUNNS.—One cup sugar, three cups milk, one cup yeast, and flour enough for a batter like common bread "sponge." Let it stand over night, then add one cup sugar, one cup of butter, one teaspoonful soda and a little lemon; mould like biscuit and let it rise again before baking.

SWEET CRACKERS.—One cup sour milk, one cup wheat meal, three-quarters cup sugar, one-half teaspoonful soda; roll thin and bake well.

QUICK PUDDING.—Three spoonfuls flour, three do. milk, three well-beaten eggs and a little salt; turn on one quart of boiling milk, and bake fifteen minutes.

CUP CAKE.—One cup molasses, one cup sour cream, three cups flour, two eggs, one teaspoonful soda.

LOAF CAKE.—One cup cream, one do. milk, one do. sugar, one egg, one teaspoonful soda ; make a thick batter with wheatmeal and bake in an oven not too hot.

PLAIN CAKE.—One cup molasses, one cup milk or cream, one-half teaspoonful soda, wheat meal to make a soft paste.

GRAHAM CAKE.—One cup sweet milk, two tablespoonfuls of cream, two of sugar, one-half teaspoonful of cream of tartar, one-fourth teaspoonful of soda; mix quite stiff with equal quantities of Graham and white flour.

HARD SUGAR CAKE.—One cup sugar, one cup butter, one cup sweet milk, one teaspoonful soda and two of cream of tartar; mix stiff enough to roll into small cakes.

COOKIES. No. 1.--One cup butter, two cups sour milk, three cups sugar, soda to sweeten the milk ; mix stiff, roll and cut in small cakes.

COOKIES. No. 2.—One cup butter, two cups sugar, one cup sour milk, one teaspoonful soda; stir in flour as stiff as can easily be stirred with a spoon, mould as little as possible, and bake in a quick oven.

DROP CAKES.--One quart flour, two eggs, one-half cup butter, one-half cup sugar, one teaspoonful soda, two teaspoonfuls cream of tartar; stir butter and sugar together, add the eggs ; mix the cream of tartar into the flour, dissolve the soda in a little milk, pour in milk enough to make as stiff as pound cake, and put in the soda the last thing ; bake in cups or muffin rings.

GRAHAM GRIDDLE CAKES.—One pint milk, one teaspoonful saleratus, one teaspoonful butter, two tablespoonfuls yeast, and a little salt; mix with Graham flour.

RICE GRIDDLE CAKES.—One pint sour milk, one egg, piece of butter half the size of an egg, soda to sweeten the milk; mix rather stiff with two-thirds cold boiled rice and one-third fine flour—boiled hominy, or cracked wheat, or oatmeal may be used in place of the rice, or equal parts of corn meal and fine flour may be used.

CORN GRIDDLE CAKE.—Scald at night half the quantity of meal you are going to use, mix the other with cold water, having it the consistency of thick batter; add a little salt and set it to rise; it will need no yeast. In the morning the cakes will be light and crisp.

WELCOME CAKE.—Stir together one and one-half cups sugar, one-half cup butter, and three eggs; sift a teaspoonful of cream of tartar and half a teaspoonful of soda with three small cups of flour; mix all together with half a cup of milk, and bake in a moderately quick oven. By adding raisins or currants a very good fruit cake may be made.

JUMBLES.—One cup butter, two sugar, four eggs, one cup milk, one teaspoonful cream of tartar, one-half teaspoonful soda; roll thin, cut, bake.

WAFER CAKE.—Two eggs beaten very lightly, one pint of cold water, one teaspoonful of salt, flour to make it as thick as fritters; bake half an hour in a hot oven, in little tins filled full; eat with butter.

BOILED WHEAT FOR DESSERT.—Pick over and wash a pint of white wheat, boil it four hours, put in salt the same as for rice; re-fill with boiling water, if more is needed; stir often the last half hour, being careful not to let it burn; cook it dry. Serve hot or cold, with sweetened cream. This is an excellent dessert and very fine for invalids.

Another very rich dish for dessert, can be made of a pint of wheat, cooked like the above, then boil in a quart of sweet milk, one cup of sugar, one cup of raisins, currants or any fruit, (raisins are preferable,) two beaten eggs; cook slowly and stir until it boils; serve cold or hot, without sauce. Or, after the wheat is washed, soak it in warm water over night, keep it wet till time for use, then simmer the water all out of it; add the milk and other ingredients, and cook as above.

ROCK CREAM.—This will be found a very ornamental as well as a delicious dish for the supper table. Boil a teacupful of the best rice till quite soft in new milk, sweeten it with powdered loaf sugar, and pile it up on a dish. Lay on it in different places square lumps of jelly or preserved fruit of any kind; beat up the whites of five eggs, with a little powdered sugar, and flavor with orange flower water or vanilla. Add to this, when beaten very stiff, about a tablespoonful of rich cream, and drop it over the rice, giving it the form of a rock of snow.

APPLE CHARLOTTE.—Take two pounds of apples, pare and core them, slice them into a pan, add one pound of loaf sugar, the juice of three lemons, and the grated rind of one. Let these boil until they become a thick mass which will take about two hours. Turn it into a mould, and serve it with thick custard or cream.

VEGETABLES.

ALL kinds of vegetables are cooked for the boarders' table as indicated in the recipes given in the fore part of this book, and are seasoned just before they are served with salt and butter; not more than a third the usual quantity employed in ordinary cooking being used.

In baking beans the salt and butter are added when they are placed in the oven.

Asparagus is cooked in pure water, taken out in vegetable dishes, and a gravy made of butter, flour and milk poured over it.

WASHING.

As cleanliness is next to godliness, a knowledge of the easiest, surest, and most economical way of following in regard to clothing the injunction to be cleanly, will not come amiss. The subjoined directions and recipes are taken from "The Laundry Manual," a little work by Mr. A. HOLLAND, an experienced launderer. It should be in the hands of every housekeeper, as the information it contains is invaluable.*

" SOAKING CLOTHES.—Whatever method of washing is adopted, previously soaking the clothes to be washed is useful; put the clothes to soak in lukewarm soap suds strong enough to raise a good lather by stirring the linen after it is put in, which should be done in some way till a good lather is produced. Sufficient water should be used to cover the linen without crowding it much, and the tub should be covered with a rug or cloth to keep the water warm as long as possible; after soaking two or three hours, or longer if convenient, the clothes should be taken out and rinsed in warm water to remove the loosened dirt before they are boiled. In this way much labor is saved as well as the wear of the linen.

Half an hour will do very well for soaking linen that is not much soiled, but when convenient it is better to let it soak longer. It is a good practice to put in soak on the afternoon previous to washing-day, and let it soak over night.

Soft water is of itself a good solvent, even of the oily materials that collect upon linen worn in contact with the body, but time is required to effect the solution. Every one is aware of the effect of keeping the hands or feet moist for a few hours—the entire external coating of secretion is dissolved. The same effect is produced by soaking for a few hours linen soiled by the excretory matter of the skin. If a little soap is rubbed on such parts as are the most soiled before putting in soak, and the linen allowed to soak from twelve to twenty-four hours, cold water will answer very well for soaking it in; but soaking linen in lukewarm water, having a little soap dissolved in it, is by far the most effectual method. Care must be taken, however, if the linen be stained, not to have the water much, if any, warmer than blood-heat, or it will set in the stains.

To save soap when the water is at all hard and will not make a lather, a portion of soda may be added to the lukewarm water: the best way of using it is to have a jug at hand, with the soda dissolved in water, and to add so much of it as is necessary to render the water soft; the quantity must be determined by experience; if too much is used it will

*For sale by MILLER & BROWNING, No. 15 Laight st., New York. Price 30 cents.

exhibit its effects upon the hands of the operator. When hard soap is used this should be dissolved in boiling water before it is added, in order to prevent any unnecessary delay in waiting for it to dissolve.

The *American Agriculturist* asserts that "the great secret of the success of nine out of ten of all the washing fluids, mixtures and machines which have been sold over the country for many years past, is owing in a great measure to the process of soaking which they invariably recommend."

"BOILING CLOTHES.—The next operation after soaking is boiling the clothes, and the water used for this purpose should be thus prepared: To ten or twelve gallons of water add half a pint of good soft soap and six ounces of sal soda, or, half a pound of sal soda and six ounces of good bar soap, and when the water is nearly or quite boiling hot and the soap and soda are entirely dissolved, put in the clothes; let them boil for twenty or thirty minutes, then, in order to produce a good color and to remove the soap and soda that have been used, which, if left in, would occasion a disagreeable smell, take them out—preserving the suds, as it can be used two or three times—and put them into a tub of clear, boiling water; then, after they have scalded for a few minutes, look them over carefully, and if you find any dirt, it can be easily washed out *without the use of a washbord.* Then rinse them in clear water, warm or cold, and they will be as white as snow.

Should the clothes to be washed require more or less than ten gallons of water to boil them in, more or less of the soap and soda can be used in proportion, or if the clothes are not much soiled, the water can be increased to twelve or fifteen gallons without using any more of the compound, provided the soap is good.*

Clothes washed by this method require no rubbing before they are boiled; for if the dirt does not come out by boiling, it will come out much more readily after boiling than before. The object of soaking the clothes is to remove the loose dirt, and thus keep it out of the boiling suds. Should the wristbands or bindings of shirts be very dirty, it may be well to rub a little soap on such parts when they are put in soak. This is all the rubbing about the whole washing, unless the clothes are very dirty, or there are any bad stains, which it may also be well to rub with soap before boiling.

By this method the finest linens, cambrics, laces, etc., can be readily and easily cleansed, and the coarsest, and dirtiest clothes readily and easily washed; and the assertion can be safely made, that it is the best and easiest mode of washing ever discovered. It certainly saves all the laborious rubbing, and enables one to complete a heavy wash in a few hours, and with very little fatigue. Washing-day is too often a day of wretchedness, ill-temper, and gloom. Everything is upset; the house is all disorder, and damp and ill-temper rule over slop and confusion. Now, if washing be a necessity, duty should make it pleasant; and the very sight of the clean white things, fluttering on the lines in the yard, should impart to the task a comfortable homeliness. We have tried many of the plans proposed to lighten the labor of washing-day. One plan promised to enable a housewife to complete a fortnight's wash in a few hours, at a cost of only five cents, and without hard labor; but in

* Poor dark-colored resin soap will not do. Any good white, or the best quality of brown soap, may be used. The less resin there is in soap the better; but the brown or yellow soap is frequently so largely adulterated with it, that it can easily be detected by its unmistakable odor. A good way to examine soap, is to rub a small piece between the thumb and finger; if poor, it will have a disagreeable, dirty, or sticky feeling.

our hands it proved a complete failure, and we have found by experience that the use of the above recipe is the best friend to the washer-woman ever invented. By it one person can do the washing for a family of ten or fifteen persons before breakfast, have the clothes out to dry, and the house kept in good order, and the gentlemen of the family, as well as all about the house, free from washing-day annoyances, and all without rubbing or machinery. Who would not wish to have such comforts?

Clothes should be divided into two or more parcels before boiling, as the dirtiest and most greasy ones ought not to be boiled with those of finer fabric containing less dirt. The finer, cleaner clothes can be boiled first, or the water for boiling the clothes in can be divided into as many parts as you have parcels of clothes, and thus boil each parcel in its proper time.

It would be well if house-keepers would always keep dirty clothes thus separated till washing-day, instead of throwing them helter-skelter into one pile or bag; for the foul air arising from the dirtiest, greasiest clothes, always injures the finer ones, and makes them more difficult to whiten. When put in soak before washing they should be separated.

Soiled or foul linen ought not to remain long unwashed, as the dirt is then more difficult to be removed. Some families wash only once a month, but once a fortnight would be better; in the meantime, as just observed; the various articles as they are soiled, should be put aside till washing-day with method, instead of being thrown together in a heap. What has been used in the kitchen and other offices should be kept separate, being generally greasy, or otherwise very foul; and, as nothing is more unwholesome, or more apt to injure the air of a house than collections of foul towels, or rags of any kind, these should, if possible, be kept in some out-house.

BLEACHING LIQUOR.—Chloride of lime five parts; sal soda six parts; boiling water half as many gallons as you have ounces of chloride of lime; put the lime into any convenient vessel, and pour about two thirds of the water on it; let it stand five or ten minutes, stirring it well; then add the soda; after the soda is dissolved, let it stand a few minutes to settle, then pour off the liquid, and add the rest of the water to the settlings; stir it well, then let it settle and pour off the liquid carefully from the dregs and strain the solution through a flannel cloth, or two thicknesses of new cotton cloth, carefully keeping out every particle of settlings. This liquor is excellent for taking out mildew and stains as well as bleaching; by exposure to air and light it loses its strength, but may be kept in well corked bottles in a dark place for any length of time; it can be used several times or until it loses its strength by exposure to air and light; most stains can be removed by soaking the linen for a few minutes in the liquid, but leather stains in cotton socks require a solution stronger than the above: it may be made twice as strong as needed for bleaching, and some kept for removing stains, and when used for bleaching it can be diluted with water.

BLEACHING CLOTHES.—After the clothes have been well washed and rinsed, they should be soaked from three to twelve hours in the bleaching liquid; then rung out, scalded, rinsed and dried. Very fine goods should not be soaked more than one or two hours. If once soaking does not render the clothes white enough, the same process may be repeated, or they can remain longer in the liquor; but it is not advisable to let them soak over twenty-four hours without rinsing and drying, as it might injure them. Soaking articles for ten or twelve hours in this liquor will take out mildew, but if there are any stains which do not come out, the stained parts should be soaked for fifteen or twenty minutes in the same liquor twice as strong as this, and then without rinsing, the articles should be soaked for a full hour in the bleaching liquid.

To REMOVE SPOTS OF GREASE OR PAINT FROM WOOLEN GARMENTS. —Wet the spot with a few drops of benzine and rub it quickly between the fingers. Oil spots and stains from candle snuffs, on woolen table covers, paint spots on garments, etc., are thus perfectly removed without the slightest discoloration.

IRON STAINS.—Dip the stained part in a solution of oxalic acid in water. The oxalate of iron thus produced, being soluble, is easily washed away. Ink spots may be removed in the same way.

Wheel-grease makes a compound stain of iron. The grease may be taken out first with alkali, then the iron with oxalic acid. If tar has been used on the wheel, rub on grease or turpentine, then apply the alkali.

INK STAINS.—Recent stains of ink may be removed if before the ink is dry the places be washed with sweet milk; if this does not succeed, rub the spots with vinegar, lemon juice or tartaric acid, and afterward wash it with soap and water. Ink or iron stains may also be removed by the bleaching liquid already described.

FRUIT STAINS.—Ammonia or spirits of hartshorn, diluted with water and applied with a sponge is excellent for this purpose. Dilute muriatic acid, two parts water to one of acid, will frequently succeed. Soak the stained parts two or three minutes, and rinse in cold water. Some faint stains may be removed by sour buttermilk. Fresh fruit stains upon calico or similar material may be removed by dipping the stained portion in boiling water."

CLEANING HAIR BRUSHES.—It is said that soda, dissolved in cold water, is better than soap and hot water. The latter very soon softens the hairs, and the rubbing completes their destruction. Soda, having an affinity for grease, cleanses the brush with very little friction.

To TAKE RUST OUT OF STEEL.—Rub well with sweet oil, and let the oil remain upon them for forty-eight hours. Then rub with leather sprinkled with unslacked lime, finely powdered, until the rust disappears.

INDELLIBLE INK.—No. 1.—Dissolve one ounce of Gallic acid in one quart soft water.

No. 2.—Dissolve one ounce of nitrate of silver in one ounce of liquid ammonia.

Dissolve half an ounce of gum arabic in half a pint of water, to which add the nitrate dissolved in ammonia. Moisten a small piece of sponge with preparation No. 1, and with it wet a place upon the garment to be marked, large enough on which to write the name. Dry it with a hot iron; then mark it with No. 2.

This is the very best ink I have ever tried, and anything marked with it can be sent to the wash within ten minutes after marking, without detriment.

www.ingramcontent.com/pod-product-compliance
Lightning Source LLC
Chambersburg PA
CBHW032122080426
42733CB00008B/1021